THE ASEAN REGION IN TRANSITION

Dedicated to the departed soul of my beloved
son who taught me how to love and that
of my father who taught me how to learn

This collection was previously published as a special issue of
The Philippine Review of Economics and Business

The ASEAN Region in Transition

A Socioeconomic Perspective

Edited by
ABU N. M. WAHID
College of Business
Tennessee State University

Routledge
Taylor & Francis Group

LONDON AND NEW YORK

First published 1997 by Ashgate Publishing

Reissued 2018 by Routledge
2 Park Square, Milton Park, Abingdon, Oxon OX14 4RN
711 Third Avenue, New York, NY 10017, USA

Routledge is an imprint of the Taylor & Francis Group, an informa business

Publisher's Note
The publisher has gone to great lengths to ensure the quality of this reprint but points out that some imperfections in the original copies may be apparent.

Disclaimer
The publisher has made every effort to trace copyright holders and welcomes correspondence from those they have been unable to contact.

A Library of Congress record exists under LC control number: 97073072

ISBN 13: 978-1-138-34156-2 (hbk)
ISBN 13: 978-0-429-44007-6 (ebk)

Contents

v

Preface

In terms of gross national product, trade, and commerce, the ASEAN (Association of South East Asian Nations) region is one of the fastest growing areas in the Asian Continent. The countries that belong to this group--are Brunei Darussalam, Indonesia, Malaysia, the Philippines, Singapore and Thailand. These countries are being rapidly transformed into urban-industrial societies. Not so long ago, all of them were very much rural-agrarian in nature, except the city state of Singapore.

By this time, significant socioeconomic progress has been achieved by these countries. One of them i.e. Singapore is already being called one of the "Four Dragons" of Asia. Its per capita GNP has exceeded that of Spain, Ireland and New Zealand. Another member of the ASEAN--Brunei Darussalam with its small population and a relatively generous endowment of oil and gas has achieved a per capita GNP quite comparable to that of Singapore.

The other countries of the ASEAN--Indonesia, Malaysia, the Philippines and Thailand have not yet experienced a major qualitative change in their socioeconomic conditions. However, if they can continue the present trend in economic growth, in near future, they are also expected to join the club of Newly Industrialized Economies (NIE) of Asia that include Hong Kong, Taiwan, South Korea and Singapore.

This collection consists of six original essays on the six member countries of the ASEAN. The first essay discusses the resource base of Brunei and the social and economic policies that the Brunei Government is pursuing in order to diversify and industrialize the economy. The second one is about Indonesia. It deals with the political and economic reforms that the Indonesian Government is undertaking to accelerate economic growth and maintain the stability of the economy. The implementation of the New Economic Policy (NEP) in Malaysia is the main theme of the third essay. It critically examines the pros and cons of NEP in the context of economic growth and racial equity. The fourth essay focuses on the government policies that are adopted to meet the current development challenges faced by the

Philippines. The fifth essay analyzes a successful role of government in the social and economic development of Singapore, where state intervention is made carefully without distorting and weakening the market mechanism. The last essay critically elaborates the conditions under which Thailand has been continually experiencing a nearly double-digit growth rate for the last decade or so.

Abu N.M. Wahid
College of Business
Tennessee State University

1 Economic and social policies of Brunei: an empirical analysis

Shamim A. Siddiqui, Abdul A. Hashim
University of Brunei Darussalam
Abu N.M. Wahid
Tennessee State University

Abstract

The discovery of oil in 1929 has been a major political and economic event in the modern history of Brunei Darussalam. After the great oil crunch of the 1973-74 and the subsequent increase in the oil price, the society and economy of Brunei entered into a threshold of transformation process. This paper is an attempt to examine and analyze this transformation process. It argues that in the midst of the transition, the prime policy goal of the government of Brunei is to diversify the economy and reduce its absolute dependence on oil and gas. In order to do that Brunei must be able to encourage the growth and development of the domestic industries without disturbing the market mechanism. At the same time, it should be able to attract direct foreign investment in Brunei by creating appropriate congenial conditions.

Introduction

Brunei is a small Southeast Asian country. It is located on the northwest coast of Borneo facing the South China Sea. The country is enclosed on the landward side by Malaysian province of Sarawak. Brunei is a mere enclave of 2,226 square miles with a population of less than 0.3 million. In 1993, the per capita GDP for Brunei was US $14,360. The history of this ancient trading *Sultanate*[1] dates back to the sixth and seventh centuries A.D. During the fourteenth and fifteenth centuries A.D., Brunei was a powerful Muslim Kingdom covering the entire land mass of Borneo stretched deep into the islands of the Philippines. In January 1, 1984, Brunei became a full-fledged independent country after almost 100 years of British protection. Soon after, in quick succession, Brunei became a member of the Association of South East Asian Nations (ASEAN), the Organization of Islamic Conference (OIC), the British Commonwealth

1

and the United Nations Organization (UNO). The country is run under the official ideology of Malay Muslim Monarchy.

The discovery of oil in 1929 has been a major political and economic event in the modern history of Brunei. Since then, the interest of the international community increased suddenly on Brunei. After the great oil crunch of the 1973-74 and the subsequent four-fold increase in the oil price, the society and the economy of Brunei entered into a threshold of rapid transformation process.

This chapter is an attempt to examine and analyze the transition that is underway in the society and economy of Brunei. It will primarily focus on the socioeconomic problems and their implications for public policy in Brunei.

A brief review of literature

The volume of literature on modern Brunei is relatively small. One of the earliest works on Brunei was done by L. W. Jones in 1966. In a section of his book, *Population of Borneo*, Jones focused on the origin, composition, current growth rate and future projections of the population of Brunei. It also briefly analyzed some rudimentary economic activities in which the people of Brunei were involved .

Nicholas Tarling in his book, *Britain, the Brooks and Brunei*, addressed the modern history of Brunei in detail. According to Tarling, the British took control of Sarawak-- formerly a part of Brunei and gained a formal influence over the *Sultan* of Brunei in 1847 through James Brook, a Victorian explorer of British origin who came to Brunei in 1838. At that time, Britain developed a trade link with Brunei. Neither Jones nor Tarling examined the socioeconomic dynamics of Brunei. In fact Brunei had been a stagnant society up until oil and gas were discovered in that land in 1929. Thereafter, trade, commerce and economic activities began to grow rapidly.

Since 1973-74, Brunei started sending diplomatic and trade representatives around the world and the society and the people of Brunei began to receive world exposure. Most of the literature available on Brunei today are government documents covering plain description of the history, society, and economy of Brunei.

The U.S. Department of State collects and publishes profile of Brunei as it does for many other countries of the world every year on a regular basis. This is a brief fact sheet about the geography, people, history, politics, economy, and trade which is used as a handy policy guide by the diplomatic decision makers. This profile does not attempt to give an in-depth analysis of the changing socioeconomic structure of Brunei. Gale Research Institute also publishes a chapter on Brunei in its, *Countries of the World and Their Leaders* series. This is subject to the same criticism as the U.S. State Department's profile on Brunei. Nigel Holloway contributed a feature to the *Far Eastern Economic Review* in 1987 on the monarchy of Brunei. This has just been a journalistic description with no depth or rigor about how monarchy works.

A major work on the economy of Brunei came out in 1986. The author-Sritua Arief, in his book, *The Brunei Economy* gave a general description of the economy of Brunei. It covers almost all sectors of the economy such as agriculture, manufacturing, trade of oil and gas, monetary institutions and the development planning of the country. The basic weakness of Arief's book is that it does not discuss the role of government and political or social forces of Brunei in shaping the manpower planning determining money supply and framing the public health policies etc.

Resource base of the Brunei economy

Oil and gas

Since the discovery of first oil field in 1929, oil and gas represent the backbone of the Brunei economy. Despite a decline over the years (83.7 percent of GDP in 1980 and 72.2 percent in 1985), its contribution to GDP was nearly 39 percent in 1993. While in the later half of 1980s, oil production was pegged at around 150,000 barrels per day, production of oil in 1993 was 170,000 barrels per day. The Brunei Shell Petroleum (BSP) in which the Brunei government is the equal partner with Royal Dutch Shell Company, has seven offshore and two onshore oil fields. Another active concession holder is Jasra-Elf, which commenced operation actively a few years ago. Almost 90 percent of its oil comes from offshore fields.

Brunei is the world's fourth largest producer of Liquefied Natural Gas (LNG) which is mainly exported to Japan. A second 20 year contract was signed in 1993 between Cold Gas of Brunei and three Japanese companies. Under this new contract, Brunei Shell will supply 5.54 million tons of LNG per annum to three Japanese power companies--Tokyo Electric Power, Tokyo Gas and Osaka Gas. Brunei's LNG plant at Lumut which is one of the largest in the world was upgraded and expanded in 1993 at a cost of B$100 million. Revenue from LNG produce is almost as significant as oil in the export and royalty profile of Brunei since the late 1970s.

The pattern of oil and gas reserves is difficult to evaluate because of lack of access to confidential data. According to a new estimate, the life of Brunei's oil reserve at the current level of production is 70 years.[2] Other conservative estimates claim that the known reserves will exhaust in 27 years.[3] On the other hand, proven natural gas reserves at the current rate of production is expected to last for another forty years.

The revenue generated by the sale of oil and gas has resulted in budget surplus over the years which has been invested in foreign countries that generates a substantial amount of income. Although, the actual amount of foreign assets is kept confidential, the London-based weekly magazine *Economist*'s "Country Profile for 1992-93" estimates the amount at US $35 billion. Furthermore, it is also asserted that the yearly income generated by these assets now surpasses the combined annual income from oil and natural gas.

3

Agriculture, forestry and fishing

The agro-economy of Brunei contributed just over 2 percent to GDP in 1993. Presently, the country imports 80 percent of its food requirements. Although land, finance and irrigation are all available and the government has established model farms to train potential farmers, the scarcity of manpower has failed to increase agricultural output and achieve even a very modest target for rice production i.e. 18 percent of the total requirement. A large supply of meat is imported from *Sultanate*'s cattle ranch in Australia[4]. There is a great potential for the development of orchards as there is a wide variety of fruits available in the country. Large scale less labor intensive, mechanized fruit plantation could be a great success in Brunei.

Forests are considered Brunei's most permanent assets. About 81 percent of total land area of Brunei is covered with diverse forest types such as mangrove, peat, swamp, heath, mixed dipterocarp and montane. Nearly 58 percent of the country is under primary forest cover. Unlike the other neighboring countries, forests have not been fully exploited for timber and other commercial uses due to the availability of revenue from hydro carbon resources. Forestry exports are prohibited by law. Under strict control of the authorities timber production is limited to 100,000 cubic meter per annum for local consumption.

Although Brunei has one of the highest consumption of sea food, its total annual sea food production is only 1,726 tons which is short of its local needs. Large areas have been identified suitable for shrimp, prawn, and fish culture. In the Sixth Five Year National Development Plan (1990-95), B$28 million has been allocated for the development of this sector.

Human resource

The total population of Brunei Darussalam was 260,000 in 1991 growing at a rate of 3 percent per annum. Out of this, the local population, including permanent residents, was 189,956 about 73 percent of the total. The local population grew at the rate of 2.5 percent during 1981-91. The Muslims, mainly Malays, constituted about 82.2 percent of local population in 1991, compared to about 77.1 percent in 1981.[5] Although the population of foreigners is about 27 percent, foreign workers constitute 37 percent of the employed labor force. Almost all foreign workers stay in the country with legal documents. The major categories of foreign workers are domestic servants, construction workers and highly qualified teachers and other professionals in the government service.

It is estimated that at present, about 35 percent of the local labor force is women which is significantly higher than many developing countries with Muslim majority. Women in Brunei take all types of jobs and play a very important role in the development of the country. The number of expatriate workers is continuously rising. At the same time, however, the unemployment rate among local population has risen from 4.82 percent in 1981 to about 7 percent in 1991.[6] This has been a cause of concern for the authorities in Brunei. It is generally understood that the main reason for this problem is mismatch.

Sectoral contribution to GDP

Table 1.1 shows the composition of gross domestic product (GDP) by kind of economic activities. It clearly exposes the role of oil sector in the economy. Although somewhat decreased, its contribution has remained significant at 38.95 percent in 1993. The decline in its share is both due to depressed international price for crude oil and government's conservation policy to rationalize the output of this exhaustible resource. The major part of the non-oil sector which is estimated to be 61.05 percent of GDP in 1993, is contributed by the government which is about 30 percent of the non-oil sector. Whatever private sector activities are there, they are still highly dependent on government activities.[7] The contribution of manufacturing sector is merely 1.7 percent and that of agriculture 1.2 percent. Social services which include education and health, both under the government, remain the most important segment of the non-oil sector.

Over the last two decades, the government has made large investments in foreign countries. A special investment agency looks after these investments but details of financial and non-financial assets and their annual returns are kept confidential. The GNP figures for the country is therefore not published by the government.

Social and welfare policies

Literacy and education

The government of Brunei Darussalam provides free education up to the university level to all its citizens and permanent residents. The country has moved toward universal literacy. This is clearly described by Figure 1.1. The definition of literacy used in 1991 was the ability of a person to read and write a simple letter or to read a newspaper column in at least one language. In terms of sex, significant differences in literacy rate has been confined to older generation i.e. age 30 and above.

However, there is a big difference between sexes for tertiary qualification. The rate of highly qualified males aged 20 and above is significantly higher than that of females. Similarly, a much higher number of males have university degrees. However, these differences are expected to narrow down given the recent trend in educational attainment.

5

Table 1.1
GDP by kind of economic activities at current prices
(totals are in million B$)

Economic activity	Year					
	1987		1990		1993*	
	Total	% of GDP	Total	% of GDP	Total	% of GDP
I Oil sector	3566.5	61.5	3490.7	53.7	2521.8	38.95
II Non-oil sector	2234.4	38.5	3017.9	46.4	3952.9	61.05
A. Government	1151.4	19.8	1436.6	22.1	1945.9	30.05
B. Private	1083.0	18.7	1581.3	24.3	2007.0	31.00
1. Agriculture	80.2	1.4	116.8	1.8	156.0	2.41
2. Forestry and logging	18.1	0.3	14.0	0.2	17.0	0.26
3. Fishing	14.0	0.2	22.9	0.4	34.2	0.53
4. Mining, quarrying, & manufacturing	123.0	2.1	177.0	2.7	—	--
5. Electrical	33.3	0.6	59.3	0.9	67.3	1.04
6. Construction	183.1	3.2	277.4	4.3	341.1	5.27
7. Wholesale trade	90.1	1.6	122.0	1.9	408.7	6.31
8. Retail trade	179.7	3.1	257.3	4.0	290.9	4.49
9. Restaurants & hotel	45.9	0.8	67.7	1.0	88.3	1.36
10. Transport storage & communications	150.4	2.6	214.1	3.3	331.5	5.12
11. Banking & finance	169.5	2.9	223.4	3.4	262.1	4.05
12. Insurance	21.2	0.4	67.0	1.0	78.0	1.20
13. Real estate & business services	59.8	1.0	65.2	1.0	74.0	1.14
14. Ownership & dwellings	37.6	0.6	55.1	0.8	73.1	1.13
15. Community, social & personal service	1126.8	19.5	1420.6	21.8	2000.2	30.89
16. Less bank charges	98.3	1.7	141.9	2.2	164.3	2.54
GDP	5800.9	100	6508.6	100	6474.7	100

*The figures for 1993 are estimates only. The contribution of mining and manufacturing units in the private sector are not available.

Source: *Brunei Darussalam Statistical Yearbook*, 1993, Statistics Division, Economic Planning Unit, Ministry of Finance, Brunei Darussalam.

Figure 1.1
Percent of the population literate by age and sex 1991
(Brunei Darussalam)

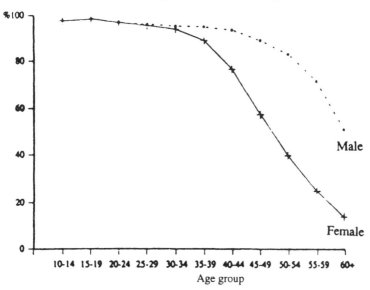

Source: *Brunei Darussalam Population Census*, 1991.

The school system is run almost entirely by the government. There are few private primary schools which mainly serve the expatriate community. A significant number of teachers in government schools is that of expatriate but the majority are locals. There are three technical colleges which award diploma in different technical and business fields. Recently a vocational school has been established to provide necessary skills to those students who are unable to complete high school education. All these technical institutions have been quite successful in producing second grade professionals and technicians. There are few local teaching staff in these colleges.

The University of Brunei Darussalam (UBD) was established in 1985 with a limited number of departments. This has allowed many school teachers to upgrade their qualifications. Furthermore, many students are admitted to the university who could not otherwise afford to go abroad on their own. Similarly, due to religious and cultural reasons, many Malay Muslim families would not have allowed their daughters to go abroad for higher education. The crude majority of the highly qualified academic staff is foreigner. However, a serious problem faced by the university is the limited number of applicants for admission and, generally with low average grades. Most of the students with good grades go abroad on government scholarships to pursue degree programs in subjects which are not offered by the University of Brunei Darussalam (UBD) such as medicine and engineering.

7

Out of 200 plus intake of UBD every year, most of them choose Bachelor of Arts or Bachelor of Science program with two main areas, one major and other as a minor. All students in this program are sponsored by the Ministry of Education which guarantees them a teaching job in government schools with a respectable salary. As mentioned earlier, because many students with good grades choose to go abroad, the entry level status of those who are accepted for admission at UBD has been relatively low. A high quality academic staff at the university certainly enhances their capability to become qualified school teachers. The Ministry of Education and the authorities at UBD are in continuous process to increase the entry level requirement to avoid a vicious circle of adding teaching staff to the school system with relatively low average grades.

Public health

Free and comprehensive health care services as well as enhanced socioeconomic environment enable Bruneians to enjoy a high standard of health. Over the decade of 1980s, the average life expectancy of Bruneians increased to 70.1 years and 72.7 years for male and female respectively. The rate of infant mortality also declined from 72.2 per 1,000 to 7.2 per 1,000 live births over the same period of time. Success of such a magnitude is indeed commendable. Other indicators are the decline in crude birth rate from 32.9 per 1,000 to 27.2 per 1,000 population, the decrease in maternal mortality from 0.38 per 1,000 to 0 per 1,000 total births. The Ministry of Health formulates the National Health Policy which is designed to give the highest level of health care and optimum quality of life to the whole population in a clean and healthy environment. Emphasis has been given to the development of a system that is based on primary health care and aimed at dispensing a wide range of benefits including preventive, curative, rehabilitative health care and support services. The main policy objectives are the reduction of infant mortality rate, disease and disabilities, and premature deaths, thereby increasing life expectancy, and control of communicable diseases.

The medical and health department under the ministry oversees the day to day management of health services through a network of hospitals, clinics, dental care centers, school health unit, mobile dispensaries, flying-doctors teams and immunization campaigns. These provisions are supplemented by Brunei Shell which has its own health plan and hospital for its employees. Private doctors, dentists and chemists are also allowed to practise after registering with the director of medical services.

Government provides free medical services to all its citizens, permanent residents, and foreigners who work for the government. Expatriate workers who work for the private firms pay at subsidized rates. Like higher education, all the hospitals are almost entirely run by foreign doctors. A significant number of paramedical staff are also

8

foreigners. One benefit of low degree of industrialization in Brunei Darussalam is that it has a very low level of environmental pollution.

Accommodation and housing

The country has seen a tremendous increase in the construction of houses during the last few decades. In 1986, only 3,900 households had no dwellings of their own. However, a third of all households still live in traditional water villages[8]. Now-a-days, these houses have modern facilities such as electricity, tap water and telephones. The very fact that they are built on river water has serious health and safety problems especially for a country with a relatively high land-man ratio and sizable financial resources. It is generally argued that the people have a preference to live in these houses. Formal studies are needed to know the real preferences and extent of adverse effect on health. If necessary, a viable program of massive resettlements should be chalked out.

As a continuing effort to raise the living standards of the people, a state wide survey in the seventies succeeded in identifying people's housing needs and eight sites where self-contained housing estates could be constructed. In addition, in the year 1984, the government launched a scheme under which a landless indigenous citizen can own a plot of land and a house at subsidized price which can be paid in easy monthly installments. The government being the biggest employer, provides its employees with subsidized accommodation and low-interest-loans for those who have land and wish to build their own houses. Brunei Shell--another big employer also provides its employees with quarters and housing loans.

Social security and old age benefits

The State Pension Division of the Welfare, Youth and Sports Ministry is directly responsible for the distribution of pensions under the State Pension Act of 1954, which became operational on January 1, 1955. The pensions are designed to give some form of financial assistance for the elderly people (60 years and above), Hansen's disease sufferers, the blind, the mentally afflicted and the disabled as well as their dependents who are citizens or permanent residents of Brunei Darussalam. Currently each pensioner is given B$ 100 per month, his/her dependents above 15 years B$ 80 and those below 15 B$ 50 subject to a maximum of B$ 500 per month per family. In 1990, B$ 10.6 million were paid to 8,700 recipients.

The state pension division also encourages jobless old age pensioners to take up handicrafts with the aim of helping them earn sideline incomes and perpetuating what they know of the country's sundry traditional crafts. The two largest employers in the country, the government and the Brunei Shell have excellent pension plans for their employees. In 1993, the government also came up with a pension plan for the private sector employees in which all the three parties involved -- the individual, the employer and the government made contributions. This was primarily initiated to make jobs in the private sector look more attractive and a drive to lessen the pressure on demand for government jobs.

Macroeconomic policies

Economic growth

In terms of economic growth, the real GDP in Brunei dollars has been declining since its boom in late 1970s when the economy grew at an average rate of about 12 percent. In the first half of 1980s, the growth rate was negative but the situation improved during the second half during which the growth rate was 4 percent. During 1990-1993 the nominal GDP grew at an average rate of 0.5 percent per annum. There are three causes of this slow down. First, the decline in the international price of oil which is the main output and export of the country. Second, the continuous appreciation of Brunei's currency with respect to US dollar. Finally, government's conservation policy of keeping the level of oil output at 150,000 barrels per day--42.5 percent lower than the peak of 261,000 barrels per day in 1979.

It should, however, be emphasized that the situation may not be as bad if we consider the possible growth in Brunei's GNP over the years. As the income from government's foreign assets--accumulated through continuous budget surplus over the years are kept confidential, the actual figure for GNP is not known. Furthermore, one should also consider the sustained improvement in the non-oil sector which has grown with an annual average rate of 10.33 percent over the last three years. It must be admitted that much of the growth in non-oil sector originates from government's direct purchase of goods and services. Furthermore, most of the activities of the non-oil private sector is also dependent on government's development program. However, as most of the government's expenditure is incurred on the improvement of infrastructure and social services such as roads, education, housing and health, it is expected that eventually the private sector will become vibrant in its own capacity.

Inflation

In spite of its development plan, substantial increases in money supply and growth in consumerism, the country has been fortunate to maintain a low level of inflation throughout the years. Table 1.2 shows the growth rate of money supply, the inflation rate and the foreign exchange rate of the Brunei dollar. The total money stock M_2 in 1993 was equal to B$3,510.4 million of which currency in circulation was 479.2 million, demand deposits B$2,031.8 million and savings deposits B$999.3 million. However, irrespective of the rate of growth of money supply, the country has been able to keep the level of prices quite stable and a low rate of inflation. One reason being

Table 1.2

Percentage growth in money supply, exchange rate and inflation

Year	Growth in money supply (M2) %	Exchange rate Brunei $ per unit U.S. $	Local bank's average prime lending rate %	Inflation rate %
1984	11.31	2.18	9.5	—
1985	3.30	2.12	8.0	2.3
1986	3.09	2.19	7.0	1.8
1987	78.61	2.01	6.5	1.3
1988	5.98	1.95	6.5	1.2
1989	6.77	1.90	6.5	1.3
1990	7.32	1.79	7.0	2.1
1991	-0.50	1.64	7.0	1.6
1992	-0.53	1.65	6.0	1.3
1993	3.53	1.61	5.75	4.3

Source: *Brunei Darussalam Statistical Yearbook*, 1993, Statistics Division, Economic Planning Unit, Ministry of Finance, Brunei Darussalam.

that Brunei has officially put its currency at par with the Singapore dollar. The later has enjoyed surplus in its balance of payments accounts over the years and is among the few countries of the world whose currency has been appreciating against the US dollar. Furthermore, in Brunei Darussalam the government has fixed the retail prices of rice, sugar and petrol and assures the availability of these essential items through its Department of State Stores and Supply which procures rice and sugar from international markets. The prices for these essential items were last revised in 1986. The appreciating Brunei currency may have helped in maintaining the prices at that level.[9]

Apart from the import of rice and sugar, the government of Brunei like that of Singapore, has a liberal import policy with low level of tariffs compared to other neighboring countries in the region. This has contributed in keeping the level of prices very stable over the years. Early this year, the government increased the import duty on cars from 20 percent across the board to a minimum of 40 percent with a maximum of 200 percent. At the same time, it decreased duties on many other consumer items including electronics and manufactured goods. As Bruneians have a very high per capita consumption of cars, the inflation rate measured by the consumers price index (CPI) has increased by 4.5 percent only in four months, January-April, 1995. It is, however, expected that this would be one time increase in price level and not a sustained increase in the rate of inflation.

Brunei Darussalam is yet to establish its central bank. The supply of money and management of the currency are presently controlled by the Brunei Currency Board. The Board's principal objective is to maintain external reserves in order to safeguard the international value of the currency and promote monetary stability. The Board also acts as the principal licensing and monitoring agency for the country's banks and finance companies. All local and foreign banks operating in the country are required to submit monthly consolidated financial reports to the Board. Currently there are nine commercial banks in the country which provide full range of banking services. Most of them are branches of foreign banks. The government of Brunei holds majority shares in Islamic Bank of Brunei which is one of the three locally incorporated banks.

The arrangement whereby Singapore and Brunei currencies are interchangeable at par continues in effect. The respective currencies are acceptable as customary tender when circulating in the country in which they are not legal tender. There are no regulatory requirements upon banks to deposit statutory reserves of any kind or of any specific liquidity requirements. Only the locally incorporated banks are required to transfer at least 20 percent of their yearly net profit to a reserve fund until it equalizes with bank's paid up capital. As far as the foreign banks are concerned, the government expects them to look toward their parent companies to provide liquidity and solvency support.

In most countries with a central bank, leading commercial banks set their prime lending rates in accordance with the discount rate. In Brunei Darussalam, the Brunei Association of Banks of which all local and foreign banks are members, fixes a uniform prime lending rate for each month in its monthly meeting. Deposit rates are also set by the Association for amounts up to B$ 100,000 and for periods up to 12 months. However, any change in the interest rate must be referred to the Ministry of Finance. In general, interest rates are set in line with those prevailing in Singapore.

In 1993 most of the loans of the commercial banks were directed toward personal loans(45.5 percent) followed by credit and finance institutions (24.9 percent), commercial units (13.2 percent) & construction industry (11.3 percent). The credit and financial institutions in Brunei are also mainly involved in personal loans. According to Standard and Poor Rating Group, the deployment of funds to loans and advancement in Brunei is low by international standards. It reflects the increasing wealth and steadily rising level of customer deposits relative to demand for credit. The high proportion of funds deployed to the inter bank market essentially represents the placement of surplus deposits by the foreign bank branches to the Singapore interbank market. The local interbank market in Brunei remains small and there is no official market for government securities in Brunei Darussalam.

It is clear that the government of Brunei Darussalam has so far not used monetary policies to its full capacity. Unlike other developing countries, it neither faces a trade deficit (or a balance of payment deficit) nor confronts an imbalance in its budgetary position. Similarly, the nature and problem of its unemployed people is different from those faced by other developing countries. It is, therefore understandable that the government has not yet felt the need for an active monetary policy. Its main concerns are limited to provide appropriate liquidity in the economy and keep price level under control.

Public finance

Table 1.3 depicts the status of revenue and expenditure profile of the government of Brunei Darussalam. The first classification on the revenue side includes import duty, income taxes, stamp and excise duties and license fees. Out of these, the significant elements are taxes and import duty. As there is no personal income tax in the country, income tax actually means corporate tax. In 1993 the volume of import duty was B$ 104.59 million whereas all other duties and license fees together were equal to a mere B$ 6.34 million. The largest amount i.e., B$ 1.029 billion came through corporate

Table 1.3
Government revenue, expenditure and budget surplus/deficit
(figures in million B$)

Revenue & expenditure			Year		
	1985	1990	1991	1992	1993
Revenue					
Total	7532.99	2796.43	2685.61	2729.57	3415.75
Duties, taxes and licenses	2578.88	1610.05	1465.50	1292.34	1143.75
Receipt for specified government services	3.9	4.41	5.08	4.91	6.46
Public enterprises	111.63	175.58	193.06	243.44	248.01
Revenue from government properties	4838.53	916.39	1021.96	1188.88	2017.52
Expenditure					
Total	4317.92	2790.49	2759.83	3057.19	3397.10
Charged expenditure	2386.74	458.02	445.75	460.15	426.03
Ordinary expenditure	1599.48	1870.50	1944.27	2136.24	2281.18
Development expenditure	331.70	461.98	369.81	460.82	689.89
Budget deficit	n.a.	22.08	105.02	266.82	45.49

Source: *Brunei Darussalam Statistical Yearbook,* Statistics Division, Economic Planning Unit, Ministry of Finance, Brunei Darussalam.

taxes. Although the details are not known, considering the poor contribution of the non-oil private corporate sector to the GDP, the bulk of these taxes come from the Brunei Shell Company of which the government is an equal partner. The largest source of revenue is the royalty received from oil and gas companies.

On the expenditure side the largest head is the ordinary expenditure which is the sum of expenditure incurred by different government ministries and departments. In 1993 the expenditure made out of this head by important sectors of the government were as follows: defense, 16.55 percent, education 12.5 percent, public works 8.48 percent, and medical and health 6.21 percent. The charged expenditure, which has declined drastically after 1985 represents expenditure incurred by His Majesty the *Sultan* of the country. The last item of expenditure is related to development projects that are mainly infrastructural.

Government budget surplus is equal to revenue *less* charged expenditure *less* ordinary expenditure *less* contribution to development expenditure *less* contribution to government trust funds *plus* capital and currency adjustments. The figure for budget deficit is not very meaningful as income from government's assets held in foreign countries is not taken into account for which no official figure is available.

It is obvious that the government of Brunei can raise more revenue by introducing personal income and wealth tax, property tax and increasing the rates of import duties comparable to those prevailing in neighboring countries. However, the availability of revenue through oil and gas sector has so far made it possible to postpone the use of these traditional sources of public finance.

Labor force and unemployment

The labor market in Brunei Darussalam is overheated with excess demand for labor in almost all spheres of the economic sectors. Excess demand also prevails in all categories of labor--skilled, semiskilled, and unskilled. Such a phenomenon is a result of the already small population base although the growth rate is relatively high averaging approximately 3.0 percent annually. Hence the local labor force has not been able to cope with the economic growth of the country even though the GDP growth rate is quite low, especially during the past decade. However, despite the overheat in the labor market, it is quite surprising to note a high number of unemployed locals. One other feature of the labor market in Brunei Darussalam is the locals' heavy dependence on the public sector for employment. A relatively higher wage level and handsome fringe benefits in the public sector compared to the private sector is the main reason for this. However, with the current awareness on the part of the government of such a problem, some active planning and execution of strategies such as wage freezing and establishment of the Workers Provident Fund for the private sector workers may reduce pressure on demand for government jobs.

A closer investigation of the labor force in Table 1.4 suggests that the male is dominant comprising 76 percent and 69 percent respectively for 1981 and 1991. Although for the intervening years labor force figures are not available, the overall annual growth rate between the years under consideration is shown to be positive at 4.7 percent--3.3 percent for the male labor force and 8.1 percent for the female. The relatively higher growth rate for the female is due to the increased number of educated females. The increased participation of females in the labor force (especially for

Table 1.4
Population, labor force and unemployment rates in Brunei 1981-91

| Index | Year | | | |
| | 1981 | | 1991 | |
	Total	Percent	Total	Percent
Population	192832	100	260482	100
Male	102942	53.4	137616	52.8
Female	89890	46.6	122866	47.2
Citizenship				
Locals	147861	76.7	189956	72.9
Foreigners	44971	23.3	70526	27.1
Labor force				
Total	70690	100	111955	100
Male	53859	76.2	75083	67
Female	16831	23.8	36872	33
Employed				
Total	68128	100	106746	100
Male	52737	77.4	72338	67.8
Female	15391	22.6	34408	32.2
Locals	43695	65.1	66602	62.4
Foreigners	24433	34.9	40144	37.6
Unemployed				
Total	2562	100	5209	100
Male	1122	43.8	2745	52.7
Female	1440	56.2	2464	47.3
Rate of unemployment		3.6		4.7

Source: *Brunei Darussalam Population Census*, 1981-91, Statistics Division, Economic Planning Unit, Ministry of Finance, Brunei Darussalam.

married females) has indirectly increased more female workers in domestic services and this again increased the economy's dependence on foreign labor.[10]

The percentage contribution of the male in employed labor force is in tandem to their contribution to the labor force, naturally! Overall in 1981, the percentage of people employed out of the total labor force is 96.4 percent and this has decreased slightly to 95.3 percent in 1991. The residual figures for 1981 and 1991, interpreted as the unemployed labor force, are 3.6 percent and 4.7 percent in that order. The degree of the economy's dependence on foreign labor could be examined from figures of employment by citizenship. In 1981, for example, 35 percent of the total employment consists of foreigners and this figure has increased to 38 percent a decade later.

The number of unemployed has increased dramatically from 2,562 in 1981 to 5,209 in 1991--a two-fold increase. The increase has posted an average annual growth rate of 7.2 percent between the years under scrutiny. It is quite interesting to note that compared to 1981, a greater fraction of male labor force was unemployed a decade later.

It is also observed that the growth rate in the unemployed male is 9.3 percent compared to only 5.5 percent for the female. Although unemployment in itself is a problem that needs serious attention, it is generally believed that the problem of disguised unemployment is a more serious problem. Such a trait is rampant not only in the public sector but also in the private sector. Apart from the direct and shorter-term consequences of under-productivity, a more perilous and destructive longer term consequences such as the over-dependence on foreign labor is also a matter that needs to be given due consideration.

International trade

Brunei Darussalam is heavily reliant on the export of non-diversified commodities--oil and gas. Likewise, for almost all its domestic consumption, it has been dependent on imported commodities. However, over the years it has enjoyed trade surplus partially due to the small population although the figures have been declining quite visibly, especially in the nineties. From Table 1.5, it could be seen that there is a large decline in its balance of trade. In 1980, for example, it stood at B$8.6 billion but within a decade this figure dropped drastically to only B$2.2 billion. The trade surplus was further declined to B$0.9 billion in 1994. One other important observation that could be gathered from Table 1.5 is the declining value of total trade. This is primarily a result of the declining export of oil and natural gas, especially that the price of oil has deteriorated over the years. Moreover, with the emphasis on resource conservation, the country has embarked upon limiting crude oil production, currently at 150,000 barrels per day. On the import side, the increase has been gradual compared to the decline in exports and therefore unable to maintain the value of total trade.

16

Table 1.5
The exports, imports and balance of trade of Brunei
(figures expressed in thousand B$)

Variable	Year						
	1980	1985	1990	1991	1992	1993	1994
Total trade	11083.5	7881.3	5823.4	6189.3	5780.0	5697.1	5880.2
Exports	9852.9	6532.9	4010.2	4266.9	3863.2	3684.5	3383.2
Imports	1230.6	1348.4	1813.2	1922.4	1916.8	2012.6	2497.0
Balance of trade	8622.3	5184.5	2197.0	2344.5	1946.4	1671.9	886.2

Source: *Brunei Darussalam Statistical Yearbook,*1993 *& Brunei Darussalam Key Indicators,* 1994, Statistics Division, Economic Planning Unit, Ministry of Finance, Brunei Darussalam.

In terms of commodities, imports of Brunei Darussalam in 1991 includes machinery and transport equipment (38.3 percent), manufactured goods (37.4 percent)and food products (12.9 percent). The main sources of imports for 1991 are Singapore, Japan, the USA, Malaysia and the UK; each comprising 22.0 percent, 15.8 percent, 13.7 percent, 9.6 percent and 7.0 percent of the total imports in that order. This pattern has not been different from that scene a decade ago. Exports destinations, too have been unchanged, with Japan leading the pack absorbing more than 60.0 percent of the total export since the early seventies (more than 70 percent then). This is followed by South Korea (10.3 percent), Thailand (8.2 percent) and Singapore (6.7 percent) according to the 1991 figures. The importance of these countries is mainly due to their import of crude petroleum and related products.

Diversification of private investment and foreign direct investment

The government of Brunei has repeatedly shown concern over the country's over dependence on oil and gas sector,[11] too much dependence on government jobs, and low level of domestic private investment.[12] In order to encourage local entrepreneurs, it established Financial Loans Scheme in 1977 under Economic Development Board (EDB). Recently, the government has also established a development bank but its function and mode of operation are yet to be made public. EDB provides loans up to B$1.5 million for a single project to local entrepreneurs at an interest rate of 4 percent. Until recently, it has granted a total of B$ 93 million. These loans were extended to people who do not work for the semi government departments. Out of the total amount, B$75 million was used for housing schemes--both commercial and residential, for rent. The reason is simple--local entrepreneurs find it safe and least complicated. Land or personnel belongings are accepted as collateral. Despite EDB's encouragement to new borrowers and for diversified activities, most applicants of new loans are the old ones and for housing projects. Every year the government allocates necessary funds to EDB to make loans for feasible projects but so far demand for loans has always been less than supply.

Probably in the hope of breaking the ice, the government established the Ministry of Industries and Primary Resources in 1988. The ministry has set up an industrial unit, specifically to help foreign investors, which houses a coordinating bureau called the One Stop Agency. The government has offered all it can to attract foreign investment in the country.[13] In the area of foreign investment, especially direct foreign investment, a clear-cut and welcoming policy could be seen in a quotation from the speech of His Majesty the *Sultan* of Brunei Darussalam:

> We have always welcomed foreign investment. We are ready and willing to look at suggestions from would-be investors. We welcome participation by major multinational companies in the economic activity of our country. Such participation would have to be on the basis of sharing the benefits equally.[14]

Up until 1985 at least, there has been an increase in real terms to B$102.2 million in non-oil private investment compared to the 1975 figure i.e. B$75 million.[15] However, this figure has declined drastically to an average of B$73 million between 1986 and 1990 (a total of B$365.4 million during the period as shown in the Sixth National Development Plan (1991-1995). As far as foreign direct investment is concerned, foreign equity investment has peaked in 1993 to B$46 million compared to only about B$5 million in 1989. In the mid-1994 foreign equity investment recorded B$27 million.[16] The cumulative foreign equity investment from the ASEAN countries is B$85 million.

Although the sources of foreign investment is diversified, the main contribution is from the United Kingdom, understandably because of Shell's involvement in oil and gas extraction. Other traditional sources include the Netherlands (association with Shell Companies) and the ASEAN countries, especially Malaysia and Singapore. Taiwan, Hongkong and Japan too are quite visible and the latter is involved in liquefied natural gas production. New investments from Japan, the United Kingdom and the Netherlands are hard to come. There are commendable investment from some ASEAN countries such as Singapore and Malaysia, and investment from Indonesia is emerging visibly.[17]

One other aspect which we would like to add with regard to the diversification policy is its effect on export and more specifically to non-oil exports. In absolute terms, there is a positive increase in the non-oil exports of the country, for example, after 1988 non-oil exports rose from B$84.6 million to B$166.6 million, a two-fold increase. However, when the country's GDP is taken into account, i.e. non-oil export as percentage of GDP, the increase is only marginal, from 1.5 percent (1988) to 2.5 percent.

In summary, tax holidays, exemption of import duty on machineries and equipments, fewer trade barriers than most neighboring countries, free exchange rate regime.[18] Minimal inflation, political stability, peace and security, availability of energy, water, telephones and good roads--all seem to make Brunei an attractive place to invest. However, so far a large part of foreign direct investment has been confined to oil and retail sectors. There are three primary reasons for this trivial response of the foreign companies. When compared to neighboring countries, Brunei has relatively high wages, scarcity of labor--especially skilled labor and its domestic market is small.

All other ASEAN countries and East Asian countries have comparative advantage in all the above areas. It appears that as far as foreign direct investment is concerned, no level of government incentive can overcome these disadvantages. It is, therefore, necessary that the country devise an endogenous development program involving local population. Another important factor of the economy of Brunei is that, relative to other communities, especially the local Chinese community, Malays are generally less inclined to take up entrepreneurial challenges. Any development plan adopted by the government must address this issue which will require multi facet research studies involving culture, sociology and existing government policies in all areas of life.

The East ASEAN Growth Area (EAGA)

In October 1992, the President of the Philippines Fidel Ramos proposed the concept of East ASEAN Growth Area (EAGA), comprising the Southern Philippines, Brunei Darussalam, East Malaysian regions of Sarawak, Sabah and Labuan and north east provinces of Indonesia. The official response of the countries involved has been very positive although there were many skeptics. Except Brunei Darussalam, the included regions of all other countries are less developed compared to the main land or core of the respective economies. There are geographical, economic and political reasons for this unbalanced development in these areas. However, it seems that all of them are now genuinely interested in improving the situation. Brunei Darussalam, which is the richest among all but too dependent on its hydro carbon deposits has joined the band wagon in the name of diversification and industrialization.

It will not be inappropriate to suggest that the idea of the EAGA has come from the success of other regional development groupings especially the growth triangle comprising Malaysia, Singapore and Indonesia. However, it is important to understand the differences between the two groupings. The driving force behind the growth triangle was Singapore's appetite for expansion and dynamism of its economy which needed more land and labor than what its own economy could provide. On the other hand, both Malaysia and Indonesia needed foreign direct investment especially in the regions close to Singapore. The private sector's desire to expand was comprehensively supported by the three governments involved who took the bold political initiative to allow both the government agencies and the private sector to take appropriate actions. Reforms were made in land acquisition and leasing procedure, movement in men and material, and provision of necessary infrastructure especially in communication and transport.

The government of Brunei Darussalam, in its pursuit to diversify and industrialize its economy, and create jobs for its increasingly educated labor force, has put too much hope to the idea of sub-regional development within the ASEAN region. The Minister for Industry and Primary Resources of Brunei has been quite busy in visiting the countries involved and signing memorandum of understanding with government agencies of the other countries as well as the private sectors.

Policy implications

It should be quite obvious from the contents of the preceding sections that the main objectives of the government of Brunei Darussalam is to stimulate the process of industrialization and diversification provide jobs to those who are currently unemployed, and create future job opportunities for its increasingly educated and trained labor force. The constraints to achieve these objectives are high cost of living compared to neighboring countries, lack of entrepreneurial dynamism among local population and the nation's implicit reluctance to further increase the dependence on foreign skilled and unskilled workers. The few manufacturing units established in the country by foreign investors have been so far successful only when they manage to employ relatively less expensive workers from neighboring countries such as the Philippines and Thailand. The effect of freezing wages in the government sector since 1984 has somehow nullified by the continuous appreciation of Brunei's currency.

Given the objectives and the constraints, there are several options worth consideration. First, the government may select few capital intensive industries for the country which can absorb local labor force and provide necessary protection through increasing tariffs for the selected items or completely banning their importation. Second, the government may decide to make Brunei Darussalam a financial hub for the region even if it has to compete with Labuan which is rapidly growing as the regional financial and banking center of east Malaysia. Finally, it is generally understood that the bulk of Brunei's foreign investment has been directed toward The United States, Europe, Singapore, and west Malaysia. The government may decide to divert some of these resources toward the growth quadrangle--the EAGA, in the shape of foreign direct investment so that a sizable number of qualified Bruneians could be employed.

Notes

1　The *Sultanate* is derived from its root *Sultan* the title of the absolute monarch of the country.

2　*Oil & Gas journal,* 28 December, 1992; Petroleum Economist, January 1993, as quoted by Mark Cleary and Simon Francis in, "Brunei: the Search for a Sustainable Economy", *South East Asian Affairs,* 1994, p. 63.

3　*Borneo Bulletin, Yearbook,* 1994-95, p. 148.

4　The government of Brunei owns a 579,000 hectare cattle ranch in Australia that is bigger in size than Brunei itself.

5　This has been calculated from Table 9.3 of the 1991 *Population Census of Brunei,* p. 81.

6　In Brunei Darussalam official unemployed rate is generally calculated by dividing number or people unemployed by total labor force which includes foreign workers. This may be misleading as foreign workers are, by definition, employed. The figures we have used in this sub-section is calculated by using local labor force.

7　See *Sixth National Development Plan,* 1991-95, p. 25.

8　A water village consists of a number of households living in houses built on water based on support poles. These houses are relatively small and are of temporary structures.

9　No official position is known in this regard.

10　Most domestic workers in Brunei come from the Philippines and Indonesia.

11　This issue of diversification has already been outlined as early as in the seventies even before the effect of the first oil price hike is felt, i.e. as outlined in the *Third Development Plan,* (1974 - 1979).

12　Also, the local private investment dependence on government investment projects in infrastructure has become a traditional behavior.

13　The latest attempt on the part of the government through the Ministry of Industry and Primary Resources in trying to boost its diversification drive is formulating the *Industrial Master Plan* in 1995. Among others, the plan has recommended a reorganization of the ministry itself, removal of bureaucratic red tape, instituting an entrepreneurs program and the development of a niche sector.

14　The Government of Brunei, *Brunei Darussalam in Profile,* 1988, p. 128, Shendwick, London.

15 Investment in the oil sector has also declined compared to the peak year figure of 1982 which stood at B$1,104 million. For example, during the *Fifth Plan* period (1986-1990) total oil sector investment was only B$1,597 million.

16 Note that these figures are exclusive of local investment and therefore may be grossly underestimated in terms of total non-oil investment. The source is the Industrial Unit of the Ministry of Industry and Primary Resources and the investment figures are for investment made in areas administered by the unit.

17 The latest, i.e. in 1993, Indonesia has invested heavily in building materials (B$38 million) and textile (B$13 million) production.

18 The Brunei currency is pegged to Singapore dollar at par.

References

Arief, S., *The Brunei Economy*, 1986, East Balmain, Australia: Rosecons.

Borneo, *Borneo Bulletin Yearbook*, 1994-95, 1994, p. 148.

Brown, D.E., *Brunei : The Structure and History of a Bornean Malay Sultanate, Brunei*, 1991, The Star Press Jalan Roberts.

Brunei Darussalam, *Statistical Yearbook*, 1993, Statistics Division, Economic Planning Unit, Ministry of Finance, Bander Seri Begawan.

Brunei Darussalam, *Brunei Darussalam Population Census* 1981-91, 1991, Statistics Division, Economic Planning Unit, Ministry of Finance, Bander Seri Begawan.

Brunei Darussalam, *Brunei Darussalam Key Indicators*, 1994, Statistics Division, Economic Planning Unit, Ministry of Finance, Bander Seri Begawan, Brunei.

Brunei Darussalam, *Sixth National Development Plan*, 1995, Bander Seri Begawan, Brunei.

Brunei Darussalam, *Third National Development Plan*, 1979, Bander Seri Begawan, Brunei.

Brunei Darussalam, *Brunei Darussalam in Profile*, 1988, Shendwick, London.

Cleary, M. and Francis, S., Brunei: the Search for a Sustainable Economy, *Southeast Asian Affairs*, 1994, p. 63.

Gale Research Institute Brunei, *Countries of the World and Their Leaders Yearbook*, 1991, Detroit, MI, U.S.A.

Hamzah, B.A., *The Oil Sultanate: Political History of Oil in Brunei Darussalam*, 1991, Kuala Lumpur: Mawaddah Enterprise Sdn. Bhd.

Holloway, N., "Model Modern Monarchy", *Far Eastern Economic Review*, Cover Story, 1987, February, 26, Hong Kong.

Johnson, O., "Labor Markets, External Developments and Unemployment in Developing Countries" in *IMF Staff Studies for the World Economic Outlook*, 1986, The IMF, Washington, D.C.

Jones, L.W., *The Population of Borneo,* 1966, The Athlone Press, London, U.K.

Singh, D.S. Rangit, *Brunei: 1839-1983, The Problems of Political Survival,* 1966.

Tarling, N., *Britain, the Brooks and Brunei,* 1987, Oxford University Press, Oxford, U.K.

U.S. Department of Commerce *Foreign Economic Trends and Their Implications for the U.S. : Brunei, International Trade Administration,* 1987, June, Washington, D.C.

U.S. Department of State, *Background Notes: Brunei,* Bureau of Public Affairs, 1991, July.

2 Policy reforms in Indonesia: a political economy perspective

Abu N.M. Wahid
Tennessee State University
Mohamad Ikhsan
University of Illinois at Urbana-Champaign
and University of Indonesia

Abstract

During the 1970s Indonesian economy grew at a rapid rate. This growth was primarily attributable to the government's oil revenue and massive expansion of public sector in Indonesia. However, the decline of oil price of the 1980s adversely affected the growth and stability of the economy. The government clearly recognized the fact that a restructuring of the economy was imperative. The present chapter is a critical analysis of this restructuring effort. It argues that the restructuring was initiated with a view to enabling the private sector and non-oil exports to play a greater role in the expansion of employment and income. The reform program began in 1983 with political and economic agenda. The political agenda includes the issues of *Pribumism* and ethnic diversity and economic nationalism while the economic agenda addressed the privatization initiative, fiscal/monetary policies and trade/investment policies. The reform process that was initiated by the government was partially successful. This chapter highlights the fact that the main reason for the reform not being fully successful is the corruption of the bureaucracy and too much political orientation of the policies.

Introduction

Throughout the 1970s, the Indonesian economy was performing well, yet some disquieting factors were prevailing there. First, on the average, the real exchange rate tended to appreciate. In conjunction with a substantial trade protection, this acted as an impediment toward export expansion. Second, a relatively high rate of inflation coupled with largely administered interest rate policy often resulted in negative real rate of interest. This, prompted capital flight and deteriorated the domestic private investment and unemployment situation in the country. Third, for much of the 1970s, rapid increase in oil revenue caused a disproportionate growth in the size and role of the public sector in Indonesia. The expanded role of public sector, combined with a strong orientation toward domestic market and a philosophy of close guidance for the private sector led to an amassment of trade and investment restrictions. As a result, the performance of supporting services, especially in the financial and the transportation sectors, were adversely affected.

In the 1980s, at the decline of the oil price and its adverse impact on the growth and stability of the economy, the Indonesian government clearly recognized that the disquieting factors constituted a major source of disturbance. It also realized that a restructuring of the economy was imperative to enable the private sector and non-oil exports to play a greater role in the expansion of employment, incomes and exports. Accordingly, the government embarked upon a comprehensive reform program in 1983 with both political and economic agenda.

The main purpose of this chapter is to analyze and examine the Indonesian reform process from a political economy point of view. It specifically focuses on the issues involving elements of the reform process, the role of domestic and foreign advisors in the implementation of the reform program and a brief evaluation of its success and failures.

Political aspects of the reform process

Agrarian radicalism and Soeharto's political strategy

One important concern of the Soeharto administration[1] is to arrest any further deterioration of economic conditions in the rural areas so as to prevent the resurrection of the Communist Party of Indonesia (PKI). In 1965, the PKI had three million members . Most of them were landless peasants living in desperate economic conditions in the countryside. Politically, Soeharto Government cannot afford a further strengthening of the PKI. And therefore, it is one of the government's priorities to improve the socio-economic status of the rural people in Indonesia and thereby prevent the growth of PKI.

Besides, President Soeharto was born and brought up in a remote rural area of Java. His childhood memory of the sufferings of the rural people of Indonesia clearly dominates his emphasis on rural development. He also strongly believes that keeping the rural people happy is a necessary though not a sufficient condition to remain in power. Because history suggests that the rural people constitute the most reliable political support base for incumbent government in third world countries.

Regionalism and regional dualism

There has been a considerable amount of dissatisfaction among a large number of Indonesians about the government's practice of discriminatory policy based on regionalism. In this regard, the critics of the Soeharto Administration allege that the inner circle of the Government is dominated by the Javanese. As a result, Java receives disproportionately large allocation of public funds for economic development while most of the resources to finance development programs come from outside Java.

This misgivings gives potential momentum to the separatist and secessionist forces in the country. In order to curb the secessionists' strength and growth, a more egalitarian regional development has been given high priority in the development planning of Indonesia. One of the justifications of the devaluation of the Indonesian rupiah is to eliminate regional disparity between Java and the rest of the country. The devaluation helps improve the terms of trade of the non-Javanese vis-à-vis Javanese. Here, it should be mentioned that the non-Javanese mainly export primary products while import substituting industries are mainly located in Java.

Pribumism[2] and ethnic diversity

There is a growing concern among the indigenous people of Indonesia about the fact that the Chinese-Indonesians' economic power is disproportionately stronger than their share in the population. Rough estimates suggest that four percent Chinese-Indonesians control about twenty percent of the resources. The *Pribumis* are outraged at this. It is widely believed that this state of affair has its root in history. Before the independence of Indonesia, the Dutch colonial policies were geared up to victimize the *Pribumis* and favor the Chinese-Indonesians. This sentiment against the Chinese-Indonesians is potentially very volatile and it erupts periodically resulting in skirmishes and riots.[3]

Policy makers in Indonesia are very skeptical about the possibility of market mechanism to resolve inequality between the *Pribumis* and the Chinese-Indonesians. They propose that Chinese domination be reduced by establishing state-owned enterprises and by adopting discriminatory policies biased toward the *Pribumis*.[4] The latter pattern gets a strong support from the nationalist groups since it creates a political patronage for them, which provides financial resources for this group.

Economic nationalism

Economic nationalism is an important factor to explain why Import Substitution Industrialization (ISI) strategy based upon largely diversified industrial base or self-reliance for industrial product becomes a popular sentiment and significant intellectual support for the Soeharto Regime. Indonesian policy makers think that they can replicate the strategy of some East Asian countries such as South Korea

27

which has been so successful in adopting the ISI at the first phase of industrialization and transformed itself into an important exporter in the world market. Indonesian authorities realize that with oil revenue and resource-based natural endowment, they can continue to maintain the ISI strategy. The main problem with this strategy is that it needs a strong commitment from the middle class and upper middle class capitalists to increase investment and productive efficiency consistently. However, due to the weak commitment, discipline and planning, Indonesia fails to adopt the second phase of the ISI strategy.

Another reason for supporting economic nationalism is based upon the rice crisis of 1972. This crisis not only induced inflation rate to 30 percent but also was the root cause of a major social crisis (riots) in the mid-1970s. The rice crisis had convinced Indonesians of the necessity of being self-reliant in rice production. Subsequently, it achieved this target in a relatively short period of time. The success story in achieving self-sufficiency in rice establishes the view that Indonesia should continue to achieve self-reliance in the production of other goods as well.

Economic aspects of the reform process

Privatization initiative

Under the reform program, Indonesia has been trying to privatize the economy slowly.[5] However, during the privatization process, many domestic activities remain in the public sector and are protected under high tariff policy. The Soeharto Administration is reluctant to release the public sector industries to the private sector for political reasons. It is keeping key industries in the government hands just to make some civil and military officials happy with the government by placing them at the top of these industries with a generous power and benefit-package. These administrators are corrupt, counterproductive and inefficient[6].

In order to protect these industries from foreign competition, high tariffs have been imposed at appropriate levels. Due to high tariff and strict government control over these industries, Indonesians are paying higher prices for the products of these industries than they can buy them in the international market.[7]

On the other hand, the financial sector is being generously liberalized with some major real sectors being heavily protected. This has been bitterly criticized as an inconsistent policy. In formulating this, the authorities are driven by political motivation rather than economic rationale.

Fiscal and monetary policies

The Indonesian government also adopts a comprehensive fiscal and monetary reform. In the fiscal area, it reduces domestic budget deficit from 8 percent of GDP in 1981-

1982 to 1-2 percent of GDP in 1985-86 by conducting tax reforms and restraint expenditure. Tax reforms have been successful reducing the dependency on oil revenue. The tax revenue now constitutes 80 percent of total revenue. In the monetary area, the Indonesian authorities have changed money supply management from direct credit to market mechanism management. Bank Indonesia has gradually reduced the liquidity credit which contributed to inflation and using the Open Market Operations in controlling money supply. On June 1, 1983, the government of Indonesia implemented financial reforms by allowing markets to determine interest rates and eliminating credit ceilings. The financial reform is being continued with abolishing entry barriers and encouraging development of money and capital markets.

Trade and investment policies

Indonesia is also adopting reform policies in trade and investment. During 1982-85, there was a reversal of the trend in the context of the reform environment. Tariff levels are now being increased. These policies are adopted not for economic justifications but for political reasons i.e. to win the political support of the domestic rent seekers in Indonesia. However, in 1986, when oil price collapsed to $8 per barrel and exchange rate realignment took place, the corrupt policy makers succeeded to convince Soeharto and his associates that they had to liberalize the real sector in order to solve the outstanding economic problems of the country. The good thing that they did was that the cumbersome customs procedures were changed. At the same time, corrupt and inefficient national customs agency was replaced by a Swiss Company for the collection of customs duties. They also simplified the rules for foreign investment in Indonesia allowing foreign ships to doc in any harbor of Indonesia. These policies have received appreciation from people of all walks of life.

The players of the Indonesian reform

Domestic advisors

There are two groups of people who have had say on the Indonesian policy reforms. The first group consists of the technocrats or economists, while second group is composed of the technicians or engineers and the nationalists. Both the groups are equally accessible to the administration and are basically opponents to each other.

The technocrats led by professor Widjojo Nitisastro[8] and Professor Ali Wardhana control the National Planning Agency, the Central Bank of Indonesia, and the Ministry of Finance. They believe in the principle of comparative advantage in trade and puts emphasis on the development of non-oil export particularly labor intensive manufacturing and agricultural products. They also believe that the "trickle down effect" works if it is combined with the Basic Needs Approach to solve the poverty problem. They use exchange rate management and monetary policies as tools to promote growth and export and control the rate of inflation.

The technocrats are not free market advocates. They believe that state intervention is the way to achieve other policy objectives besides economic efficiency. Though their influence continued to grow over the government machineries up until the early 1990s, these technocrats have never had the kind of authoritative autonomy as enjoyed by their counterparts in Singapore. They have only a little control over some strategic industries such as *Pertamina* (state oil company) or *Bulog* (good agency). They share power with civilian and military rivals who have different views on development strategy. Since their rivals have the control over the portfolio positions, many policies formulated by them have not been implemented by their rivals. The technocrats' relationship with the Soeharto Administration is such that when an economic crisis breaks out, the government seeks their advice and when the problem is over, the government ignores the technocrats.

The opponents of the technocrats are the technicians and the nationalists. Their principal leader is Habibie--the Cabinet Minister for Technology Affairs. Habibie's followers include technician-cum-managers, military advisors, and some economists, mustered by their belief in general validity of the infant industry arguments and dislike of foreign ownership of capital. The technicians and the nationalists hold the view that the development of state enterprise is a way to balance the Chinese domination of the private corporate sectors in Indonesia. The anti-Habibie group, i.e. the technocrats also control the Ministry of Trade, the Ministry of Industry and the National Investment Coordinating Board. They are in favor of expanding domestic manufacturing sector, including making airplanes. They believe in the Big Push Theory and recognizes the legitimacy of state intervention in the development of strategic industries. Even though the Habibie followers are opposed to the technocrats, there are some differences among themselves. The technicians emphasize on high technology growth while the nationalists are committed to equity-based growth.

Foreign consultants

Since the oil boom of 1973, the number of foreign consultants in Indonesia had increased significantly. Unfortunately, not all of them were of high quality and some of their works and recommendations were quite trivial and had reflected their inadequate knowledge and understanding of the Indonesian issues. However, to be fair, there are many cases where they produce some truly innovative works. Some policy reforms such as price stabilization initiative of the 1970s, fiscal and financial reforms of the 1980s have been quite commendable.

The World Bank and the IMF had significant contributions to the implementation of the economic aspects of the reform package in Indonesia. The domestic critics allege that the Indonesian authorities has sold the country's independence and sovereignty to the World Bank/IMF experts and follows their dictations fully in making the reform policy. However, the observers with international agencies assert that the Indonesian policy makers are stubborn and hardly pays any attention to what the the World Bank/IMF experts have to say.

It is not clear, how independent the Indonesian authorities are in formulating the reform policies. However, there is no doubt that the reform package they put together is a result of their 25 years of learning the Indonesian development process. Thus, the idea of economic reforms in Indonesia might have been in place well before the IMF and the World Bank advisors had arrived.

Positive impact of the reform

On growth

Indonesia had succeeded to avoid a recession during 1982-83 and to follow a sustainable growth path as a result of the reform process. The economic growth moved from a five-percent path in 1983-86 to a six-percent path in 1986-90 and recently rose to nearly a seven-percent path during 1990-93 as shown in Table 2.1.

More interestingly, Indonesia also succeeded to avoid repercussion effect of recession that prevailed in industrialized countries in the 1980s. There are two reasons for this success. First, it could effectively diversify the export market and second, strong growth and more equitable distribution of income had boosted domestic demand. Since 1990, domestic demand contributed more than 60 percent of GDP growth.[9] On balance, the growth in Indonesia is attributable to significant increase in

Table 2.1
Growth in GDP and some selected sectors of the Indonesian economy
1980-93 (percent per annum)

Measures	Before the reforms	During the reform years		
	1983-86	1983-86	1986-90	1990-93
GDP	3.2	5.1	6.4	6.8
Oil	-4.0	3.3	2.5	2.9
Agriculture	2.6	3.7	3.4	3.5
Mining	-4.0	0.4	1.8	3.9
Manufacturing	3.6	14.0	11.0	10.7
Construction	6.1	0.1	10.0	10.2
Electricity	19.0	11.0	14.0	12.1
Services	8.2	5.8	7.4	7.3

Sources: CBS, the World Bank, Bank Indonesia and authors' estimates.

availability of capital and improvement in the level of overall efficiency of the economy. Compared to the pre-reform situation, oil and mining sectors grew significantly in the early 1990s. However, as the reform process was underway, these two sectors lost their relative importance in the overall economy. During the reform period, the growth rate in the oil and mining sector either remained stable or declined slightly.

Agriculture, Manufacturing and construction sectors recorded significant improvement in their growth rates. This reflects a structural shift in the economy from the traditional oil to non-oil sectors. Surprisingly, we observe that the services sector demonstrates a slight decline. The decline in the electricity sector may be explained at least partially by the fact that it has been under the control of the corrupt and inefficient Soeharto family.

On mobilization of savings

Table 2.2 shows that economic reforms left a positive impact on the domestic savings mobilization in Indonesia. Financial reforms have produced some positive impacts on gross national savings that has increased to an East Asian level.

Estimating private consumption as a function of aggregate disposable income, real rate of interest and lagged private consumption, Ikhsan[10] showed that the financial reform in Indonesia increased the real rate of interest and thereby induced domestic private savings significantly. He also showed that the financial deepening indicator (M2/GDP) had risen significantly from 17.7 percent in 1982 to 40 percent in 1992. It not only reduced capital flight but also prompted repatriation of some capital flight.[11] Figure 2.1 vividly describes this fact.

In a separate study, Hanna[12] demonstrated that financial reform produced a positive impact on efficiency of savings mobilization in Indonesia. However, due to restrictions and distortions in the real sector of the economy, private investors did not expand their business activities but put their profit into the bank to get higher return

Table 2.2
Mobilization of savings in Indonesia 1983-93 (percent per annum)

Measures	Before the reforms	During the reform years		
	1983-86	1986-90	1990-93	1980-83
Gross national savings	23	23	32	33
Private savings	11	15	22	20
Public savings	12	8	10	13

Source: Same as Table 2.1.

Figure 2.1
Capital flight in Indonesia 1970-91

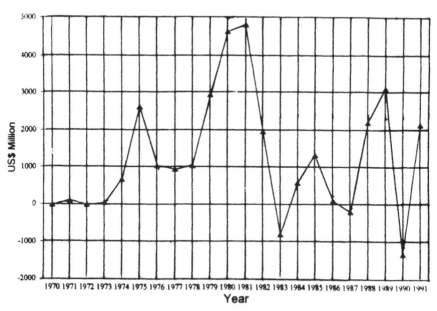

Source: Authors' calculation

with lower risks. It seems that this situation occurred in 1983-1986 when domestic private investment grew by only 4.1 percent per annum. However, on the wake of the real sector reform that began in 1986, private investment spurred to 25 percent per annum and resulted in high increases in GDP. This finding implies that sequencing of economic reform is important. When financial sector was reformed while real sector was protected, the reform results were gloomy and financial crisis prevailed in the Indonesian economy.

On aggregate economic efficiency

The overall level of economic efficiency was also improved as a result of the reform process. This is depicted in Table 2.3. All aggregate efficiency indicators such as Incremental Capital Output Ratio (ICOR), Aggregate Rate of Return (Y/I) and Total Factor Productivity (TFP) show persistent improvement. Dasgupta, Hanson and Hulu[13] found that during 1986-92, 30 percent of GDP per worker was due to increase in TFP, while 55 percent was due to increase in physical capital and the remainder due to improvements in human capital.

There are some possible reasons that led to improvements in efficiency during the reform period. First, devaluation of rupiah has corrected relative price ratio and

33

Table 2.3
Aggregate efficiency measures in Indonesia

Measure	Before the reform	During the reform years	
	1973-81	1982-85	1986-90
Rate of return			
on investment	31.4	13.1	29.5
ICOR	2.8	7.8	3.9
Percent change in TFP (p.a)			
Input growth	7.1	7.0	4.8
Capital stock	10.7	9.8	6.7
Labor	3.0	2.8	2.5
TFP growth	0.9	-2.5	2.6
Non-oil GDP growth	8.0	4.0	7.4

Source: Authors' calculation and World Bank's staff estimates.

reduced the imported capital goods prices. Second, along with financial reforms, devaluation also corrected wage-capital ratio and induced the economy toward more labor intensive in which Indonesia has comparative advantage. Third, financial reforms have removed distortion in the financial market and induced more efficient use of capital. Fourth, trade reforms created a more competitive environment and made only the efficient industries survive. Trade reforms also allowed the domestic industries to exploit economies of scale to a great extent.

On labor productivity

The Rapid transformation of the manufacturing sector from inward to outward orientation, generated strong growth and labor productivity. Manufacturing employment grew by 7 percent per annum compared to 2.5 percent for the whole economy and contributing directly for 30 percent of the total increase in employment during 1985-90. Labor productivity in manufacturing rose impressively during 1985-90 averaging 6.6 percent per annum compared to 3.6 percent for the economy as a whole. However, real wages in manufacturing sector increased only 2.6 percent per annum during the same period.

On income distribution

These reform policies have done a remarkable job in ensuring that the benefit of economic development are widely shared. One aspect of this trend in the incidence of poverty. The incidence of poverty had reduced to only 13.7 percent--about

25.2 million people in 1993 compared to about 54 million people in 1976. Other indicators also show considerable improvement. The share of consumption expenditure of the poorest quintile of population has increased from 6.9 percent in 1970 to 8.9 percent in 1990. Compared to other developing countries, this record is relatively high. In Malaysia the share of lowest quintile accounted only 4.6 percent, in the Philippines only 5.5 percent while in Sri Lanka only 4.6 percent. Data on official Gini Coefficient also show an improvement in distribution of income. Gini Coefficient has declined from 0.38 in 1978 to 0.33 in 1993. Finally, during periods of adjustment, i.e. 1984-90, income per capita grew at 3.7 percent. Per capita income rose more rapidly in rural areas than in urban areas during this period. These all indicate Indonesia's growth has benefited the lower income group.[14]

The downside of the reform process

Failure to control inflation

Even though the reform program produces many good results, yet Indonesian economy suffers from several structural problems. One such problems facing the country is the inability of the government of Indonesia to reduce the rate of inflation to a target of 5 percent per annum. High inflation rate is not only bad for the domestic political economy of the country but also makes the country less competitive in the world market. Soaring inflation rate makes Indonesia loses its export market to the competing neighbors--Thailand and Malaysia.

As to combating inflation in Indonesia, we first need to know the source of inflation i.e. whether it is coming from excessive aggregate demand or from some structural deformities of the economy. Using a structuralist-monetarist inflation model, Ikhsan[15] estimated the inflation equation using annual data for 1973-92 and found that both cost push and demand pull factors had contributed to inflation in Indonesia.

Using Beta Coefficient, one may calculate which factors contributed more to inflation rates. Estimation results both using GDP deflator and CPI as indicators of inflation showed that 70 percent of inflation was caused by increases in rice price as expected wage and imported inflation. Only 30 percent is caused by demand factors such as output gap and money supply growth and fiscal deficit. This suggests that demand management cannot be used as policy tool to combat inflation rates. The government should use structural reforms in order to relax the existing rigidities in domestic markets.

Remnants of protectionism

In spite of significant progress in liberalizing trade policies, effective rate of protection (ERP) represented by net effect of tariff and non-tariff barriers still remain high in Indonesia. According to Table 2.4, ERP for the manufacturing sector was as high as 52 percent in 1992. ERP of similar magnitude was found with the agricultural sector as well. It is worth noting that whenever a substantial reductions in protections have taken place, the competitive position of the affected sector has improved.

For example, reduction in the tariff in textile and garment industries in combination with deregulation in cotton import have reduced ERP from 102 percent in 1987 to 34 percent in 1992 and have boosted export of this commodity by more than 30 percent per annum during 1987-92. In many other subsectors, including food processing, paper, non-metal products, automotive and engineering industries, ERP still remains high. Trade policies thus continue to be severely biased against export. In addition to protecting high cost domestic industries from competition, these policies are against the objective of stimulating non-oil export growth.

Bottlenecks with economic infrastructure

Another problem with the supply side is that there are some bottlenecks in infrastructure such as electricity, roads, harbors, telecommunications etc. not only in availability but also in reliability. This is because of the availability of limited funds to finance infrastructure development and existence of state-monopoly or quasi-state-monopoly in infrastructure services in Indonesia. Inefficiency of state owned enterprises in operating infrastructure services is not only due to internal inefficiency

Table 2.4
The Structure of effective rate of protection (ERP) in Indonesia

Economic sector	ERP		
	1987	1990	1992
Manufacturing	68	59	52
Food	122	126	120
Textile	102	35	34
Wood and wood product	25	33	33
Paper	31	20	20
Chemical	14	13	12
Non- metal	57	49	44
Metal	13	10	10
Metal product	152	139	82
Others	124	79	80
Import-competing	39	35	32
Export-competing	-2	-1	-1
Anti-trade bias	41	36	33

Source: The World Bank's staff estimates.

but also of external pressures. For example, generation and distribution of electricity in Indonesia is under the control of the Soeharto family. Just because of the Soeharto connection, it is still in business even though it is 20 to 25 percent less cost effective compared to its counterparts in Thailand and Malaysia.[16]

Regulation in the banking sector

The efficiency and robustness of a financial system depend on the quality and efficacy of regulatory and legal framework under which the system operates. Efficient financial intermediation requires access to reliable information on borrowers which in turn necessitates clearly a defined standard and auditing requirement. The Indonesian financial system, at present, falls short of many such requirements. The introduction of so-called Prudential Banking Regulation has limited the capacity of authorities to effectively supervise financial institutions and regulate the money/capital market properly.

Inadequate laws governing the financial sector, lack of reliable information on borrowers, absence of proper accounting and auditing requirements and unenforceable security and collateral practices have not only increased the cost of doing business in Indonesia, but also has resulted in concentration of credit in a small number of business groups. Concentration has been further perpetuated by the unscrupulous lending practices of state-owned banks in favor of large groups who hold strong political power in Indonesia. These practices are often in violation of legal lending limits, and the interlocking between banks and the real sector. An unpublished study by the World Bank showed in 1992 that 76 percent of the loan disbursements by state-owned banks went to the large business groups, whereas other domestic private banks distributed only 54 percent of their loans to these large groups. The study also showed that the large groups had a high debt equity ratio, i.e., 202 percent as opposed to 28 percent and 44 percent for small and medium size companies respectively.

The financial system in Indonesia has other important weaknesses particularly in long term financing. The capital market is developing but it is limited in size and depth. Indonesia's capital markets are one of the smallest in Asia, in terms of the number of companies listed, market capitalization, trading value and turnover etc. In banking sector, we find mismatches in maturity terms for the source and use of funds. The maturity of funds has been declining because of reduction in the share of demand deposits, and on the other hand, share of time deposits has increased. In addition, maturity of time deposits is also shortened. However, maturity of credit demanded has been lengthened in line with the transformation of Indonesia's economy. This mismatch has made a serious problem to the firms in financing their projects. They may rollover their loans but any changing terms of credit--because of unfavorable macroeconomic environment toward unfavorable terms of credit may hurt them. This in turn makes them fail to pay their obligations. These structural problems have produced a fragile financial system on which depositors put a very high risk premium.

Concluding remarks

Despite some undesirable outcomes, on balance, the policy reforms in Indonesia may be considered as a step forward toward economic growth, stability and equity. From institutional point of view, it has also produced some interesting results. Although the role of the technocrats in Indonesian policy making recently eroded, their view of economic deregulation gained significant support from other quarters who were previously opposed to deregulation.

It is widely believed in Indonesia that deregulating could be a major policy instrument to maintain long-term competitiveness in the international market and sustain growth in income and employment. With the protection regime in place now, the agriculture in Indonesia cannot expand further because all Indonesian agro-based industries are lagging behind those of Thailand and Malaysia. Despite the fact that Indonesian agriculture enjoys advantage compared to those of Thailand and Malaysia, the protectionist policy of providing subsidized inputs to the agricultural products such as sugarcane, wheat, soybean etc. cannot make them economically viable.

The traditional power structure in the rural areas and a vested interest group has been quite critical about the reform process. The reform, at least to some degree, has ushered redistribution of income and power in favor of those who were hitherto left out from all sorts of development activities. The vested interest group did not or could not adjust themselves to this dynamics and are therefore unhappy with the reform program.

Another reason for some people to oppose the reform program is social jealousy. Among them, wide-spread belief exists that the reform process has overwhelmingly benefitted the Chinese-Indonesian capitalists. That is true and inevitable. Because, objective analysis suggests that the Chinese-Indonesians are far more efficient and enterprising in business than those of the *Pribumis*. Over and above, the Chinese-Indonesian capitalists are adept in using the political leverage of the coalition between Chinese-Indonesian military or Chinese-Indonesian bureaucrats toward fulfilling their business goals. This group has a very effective lobby in the Soeharto Administration as well. The reform policy suffers another major set back due to the internal strifes, corruption and week personality of the reformers themselves. They also provide unscrupulous support to Soeharto's friends and family in their rent seeking activities. Some members of the reform group also get involved in family business in which there are clear cases of conflict of interests. Some of them also are indicated of being involved in the two big scandal in banking sector consisting of one private bank and one state owned bank. All these negative elements threaten the prospect of deregulation in 1990s.[17]

During the 1993-98 term of his presidency, Soeharto wants to change his development strategy. His removal of the technocrats from Central Planning Agency and limited their authority to just monetary and financial affairs produced repercussions in the private sector. Private sector does not seem to be happy with this decision. Sudden plunge in the stock market index and rise of short-term interest bear testimony to this fact. The president responded quickly by reassigning the two important leaders of the technocrats--Widjojo Nitisastro and Ali Wardhana as the president's economic advisors. Thus the sustainability and success of economic reforms in the 1990s will depend on the political will of the Soeharto Regime which is often driven by the interest of the business of his family and close associates. Soeharto is reluctant to reduce the protection of his friends and family. And thus the business community at large is skeptical about the future of the reform process in Indonesia.

Notes

1   The present government.

2   The *Prebumis* are the indigenous people of Indonesia. The concept of *Prebumism* represents government policies favoring the Prebumis over the Chinese-Indonesians.

3   The racial riots against Chinese-Indonesians have occurred several times. In the early 1970s, in Bandung, a racial riot broke out because a Chinese-Indonesian had a traffic accident with an indigenous beca driver. This riot had spread out all over Java and resulted in callosal loss of lives and properties of both the *Pribumis* and the Chinese-Indonesians. The 1994 labor riot in Medan of North Sumatra also originated from racial tensions resulting in the death of some Chinese-Indonesian businessmen.

4   The Indonesian government's policy of providing special favors to the Pribumi businessmen virtually failed. Many unscrupulous Chinese businessmen got advantage of it just by showing a Pribumi director of their businesses.

5   Privatization of the State Owned Enterprises (SOEs) in Indonesia includes selling 10-15 percent of their shares to the public. The objective is to pay-off the foreign debt.

6   Generation and distribution of electricity was kept in the public sector to be headed by the Soeharto family. They prove themselves to be so inefficient in managing this industry that its production cost is about 20 percent more than its counterparts in Malaysia and Thailand.

7   Examples are sugar and wheat flour. In Indonesia, prices of sugar and wheat flour are about 75 - 38 percent higher than those of the world market respectively.

8   Professor Nitisastro served as minister in Soeharto's cabinet from 1966 and from 1978 up until now serving as Soeharto's economic advisor.

9   A. Anwar and I. Azis, "Short Term Prospect of Indonesian Economy-1994-96", in Arsjad Anwar (ed), *Prospek Ekoomia Indonesia Jangka Pendek: Peranan Sumber Saya Manusia dan Teknologi*, 1995, Jakarta: PT Gramedia and FEUI, Bahasa, Indonesia.

10   M. Ikhsan, *Interest Rates, Exchange Rates and the Role of Monetary Policy After Financial Reforms: The Case of Indonesia*, 1983-89, 1991, M.A. Thesis, Vanderbilt University, Nashville, USA.

11   Capital flight is measured by non-official short-term capital flows.

12   D. Hanna, "Indonesian Experience with Financial Sector Reform", *World Bank Discussions Paper*, 1994, No. 237, Washington, D.C.

13   D. Dasgupta, J. Hanson and E. Hulu, "The Rise in Total Factor Productivity During Deregulation: Indonesia, 1985-92", paper presented in the conference, *Building on Success: Maximizing the Gains from Deregulation*, 1995, Jakarta.

14   Despite the increase in the travel cost to Mecca for pilgrimage, a significant increase in the number of rural people wanting to go for pilgrimage at least partially validates this fact.

15   M. Ikhsan, 1991, op. cit.

16   The World Bank, *Indonesia: Public Expenditures, Prices and the Poor*, 1993, Washington, D.C.

17   For details, see A. Schwarz, *A Nation in Waiting: Indonesia in the 1990s*, 1994, Westview Press, Boulder, CO.

References

Ahmad, S. and Chibber, A., "How Can Indonesia Maintain Credit Worthiness and Non Inflationary Growth?", *World Bank PER Working Paper*, September 1989.

Anwar, M. A., and Iwan J. A., Short-Term Prospect of Indonesian Economy, 1994-1996 in M. A. Anwar et al (eds), *Prospek Ekonomi Indonesia Jangka Pendek: Sumber Daya Manusia dan Teknologi*, Jakarta: PT Gramedia and FEUI, 1995, in Bahasa Indonesia.

Azis, I. J., "Indonesia", in J. Williamson (ed), *The Political Economy of Policy Reform*, 1994, Washington DC, Institute for International Economics.

Dasgupta, D., James, H. and Hulu, E. "The Rise in Total Factor Productivity During Deregulation: Indonesia, 1985-1992", paper presented in the conference, *Building on Success: Maximizing the Gains from Deregulation*, Jakarta April, 26-28, 1995.

Haggard, S. and Webb, S. B. (eds.), *Voting for Reform: Democracy, Political Liberalization and Economic Adjustment*, 1995, New York: World Bank and Oxford University Press.

Hanna, D. P, "Indonesian Experience with Financial Sector Reform", *World Bank Discussion Paper*, 1994, No. 237, The World Bank, Washington, D.C.

Ikhsan, M., *Interest Rates, The Exchange Rate and The Role of Monetary Policy After Financial Reforms: A Case of Indonesia*, 1983-1989, *MA Thesis*, 1991, Vanderbilt University, Nashville, USA.

Schwarz, A., *A Nation in Waiting: Indonesia in the 1990s*, 1994, Westview Press, Boulder, CO.

World Bank, *Stability, Growth and Equity in Repelita* VI, Report No. 1994, 12857-Ind.

------- *Indonesia: Sustaining Development*, A Country Report, 1994.

------- *Indonesia: Public Expenditures*, Prices and The Poor, 1993.

------- *Indonesia: Industrial Policy-Shifting into High Gear*, June 1993.

3 Malaysia in transition[1]

Anis Chowdhury
University of Western Sydney--Macarthur

Abstract

The Malaysian economy has undergone rapid transformation within a short span of two decades and has a vision to become a fully developed economy by the year 2020. This chapter provides a brief synopsis of this remarkable growth and structural change within Malaysia's historical and political developments. It also highlights the problems associated with rapid transformation. The chapter argues that the spectacular transformation of the economy cannot be explained by the conventional wisdom of either neo-classical variety or statist paradigm. The chapter attributes much of Malaysia's success to its racial compact at the time of independence and the subsequent pursuit of New Economic Policy which aimed at racial and political harmony within the context of a growing economy. How successfully Malaysia can move toward an "innovation driven" society will depend very much on its success at political reforms toward a more open and plural system.

Introduction

Malaysia, the star performer among the South East Asian nations, has posted a sustained high growth rate of around 9 percent per annum for eight years in a row (1988-1995). The result have been a spectacular rise in gross domestic product (GDP) per capita, estimated at US$2,581 in 1991, and a rapid structural change. The share of manufacturing in GDP rose from 15 percent in 1970 to a staggering 40 percent in 1993, qualifying Malaysia as an industrialised or at least a next-tier newly industrialising economy (NIE). This rapid transition of Malaysia from an agricultural and resource-based economy to an NIE defies the conventional East Asian development paradigm which relies either on cultural determinism (so called Confucianism) or on strong state autonomous from narrow interest groups. This chapter seeks to locate Malaysia's transition within a political economy framework and attributes much of its success to the concept of "shared growth" enshrined in the

43

New Economic Policy (NEP) designed to balance the economic interests of dominant racial groups. It begins with a brief outline of Malaysia's history and political developments followed by a snap-shot of its economic transition. The importance of NEP can be better understood within a historical and political context that has shaped modern Malaysia.

History and political developments[2]

The modern Malaysia came into existence after gaining political independence from the British rule on August 31, 1957. It consists of 11 states in Peninsular Malaya and 2 states in the island of Borneo. However, its historical roots lie in the founding of Malacca *Sultanate* (Kingdom) in 1400 AD. Malacca was a vigorous trading and cultural one million which influenced the shaping of political institutions and traditional Malay culture through the succeeding centuries. Malacca was captured by the Portuguese in 1511 and subsequently by the Dutch in 1641. The colonial powers attempted to prevent the rise of another Malay state in the peninsula which could rival the distinction of Malacca. By the mid-18th century the modern geopolitical pattern of Malay states emerged in the peninsula beyond the influence of European fortified entrepot of Malacca.

In an attempt to secure the trade route to China through the Straits of Malacca, the British captured the Island of Penang in 1786 and Malacca in 1795. Following the establishment of a trading post in Singapore in 1819, the British formed a single administrative unit, the Straits Settlements in 1826 comprising Penang, Malacca and Singapore. The Straits Settlements were administered from British India until 1867 when the administration was transferred to the colonial office in London.

Although initially the British did not want to involve in the Malay states, the rivalry among Malay rulers following the discovery of major tin deposits in Perak and other mining activities slowly drew the Straits Settlements into closer political and economic ties with its hinterland. As the Malay rulers fought among themselves often using the secret societies of migrant Chinese workers to control newly found wealth, there was total collapse of law and order by the late 1860s. The local Chinese and European merchants urged the Straits Settlements to intervene and restore order. In 1873 the British Government agreed to intervene in the fear that the chaos would give the rival German colonial power an opportunity to capture the peninsula, threatening its commercial interests. Over the period 1874-88, the British entered into agreements with the Malay rulers of Perak, Selangor, Negri Sembilan and Pahang, which required the *Sultans* (Kings) to accept a British Resident whose advice 'must be asked and acted upon on all questions other than those touching Malay religion and custom'. The *Sultans* were allowed to keep all their privileges and splendour of Malay ceremonial court. This agreement effectively turned the Malay rulers figure heads while the executive powers rested on the British Resident.

A Federated Malay States (FMS) with the four signatory states was established in 1896 and Kuala Lumpur became its capital. By 1914 four northern states of Kedah, Perlis, Kelantan and Trengganu and the southern states of Johor accepted permanent British advisers. Although these five states remained outside the FMS and became collectively known as Unfederated Malay States (UMS), the acceptance of permanent British resident advisers effectively allowed the British rule to extend throughout the Malay peninsula.

The British rule was interrupted by Japanese occupation during 1942-45. After the Japanese surrender, the British began negotiations with a new political force, United Malays National Organisation (UMNO), and the Malaya rulers to form a unified administration of Malayan Union, combining FMS, UMS, Penang and Malacca. This eventuated in the formation of the Federation of Malaya in February 1948. The new constitution of the Federation maintained the sovereignty of *Sultans* and granted citizenships to the Chinese and Indian settlers.

The restrictive citizenship requirements for the Chinese and Indians angered the non-Malay settlers, in particular the Chinese regarded the Federation as a betrayal of the loyalty they had shown to the British during the Japanese occupation. This strengthened the hardliners in the Communist Party of Malaya (CPM) which launched a guerilla warfare against the colonial rule. However, the CPM did not enjoy much support among the Malays and by the mid-1950s the communist insurgency died down.

By then, however, the British decided to grant self-government to the Federation and worked toward finding a consensus among the various ethnic groups. The negotiation among the various groups resulted in a compromise whereby the Malays retained the political power and in exchange allowed the Chinese to continue their economic functions with the understanding that in time more equality would be achieved among the races in both economic and political spheres. The new constitution also had the provision for a single nationality, with citizenship open to all those in Malaya who qualified either by birth or by fulfilling requirements of residence and language. Independence was proclaimed on August 31, 1957 and the Umno President, Tunku Abdul Rahman became the first Prime Minister. The government was formed by the coalition of major ethnic oriented parties UMNO, the Malayan Chinese Association (MCA) and the Malayan Indian Congress (MIC).

Singapore joined the Federation of Malaya in 1963 when it gained full independence. But in order to prevent the Chinese becoming numerical majority with Singapore's entry, Sarawak and North Borneo (renamed Sabah) were also taken into the Federation to form the Federation of Malaysia. However, Singapore's membership was always an uneasy one due to its more "radical" politics and Lee Kuan Yew's intention to participate in the politics of the mainland. Singapore was, thus, expelled from the Federation in 1965.

The formation of the Federation of Malaysia was not taken very easily by Indonesia and the Philippines which had laid its territorial claim to the North Borneo (Sabah).

In 1963 both Indonesia and Philippines broke off diplomatic relations with Malaysia and Indonesia launched a series of military confrontations. However, after the failed coup in Indonesia in 1965 and Soeharto's accession to presidency, the tension eased. Later the formation of the Association of South East Asian Nations (ASEAN) in 1967, a quasi-security arrangement against the advancing communists, helped improve Malaysia's relations with both Indonesia and the Philippines greatly.

Malaysia is a multicultural society where the indigenous Malays interacted with the Chinese, Indians and other cultures ever since the spice trade flourished along the prosperous maritime trade route linking China and India thorough South-East Asia. The Arab traders brought Islam and the majority of Malays are Muslims. The Chinese and Indians migrated mainly during the colonial period to work in plantations and mines. In the Peninsular Malaysia, the Malays constitute about 59 percent of the population, the Chinese 31 percent and Indians 10 percent. In Sabah and Sarawak, the Chinese population comprise about 14 percent and 29 percent respectively. Despite a long history of interactions among the Malays, Chinese and Indians, a common culture did not emerge and each group maintained more or less their distinct ethnic and cultural identity. The division of economic functions along ethnic lines was largely responsible for mutual distrust and perhaps prevented cultural integration to some extent.

Political developments

Malaysia is a Parliamentary democracy with a figure head monarch and executive parliament, elected by popular votes. The conference of independent Malay rulers (*Sultans*) elect the Monarch (*Yang di-Pertuan Agong*) from among themselves. The current Monarch (elected in 1994) is Tunku Ja'afar ibni Al-Marhum Tunku Abdul Rahman, the Sultan of Negri Sembilan. The *Sultan* of Selangor is his deputy.

Political developments in Malaysia are driven primarily by ethnic tensions and compromises. Malaysia since its independence is ruled by a government of coalition among UMNO, MCA and MIC - the three major parties representing Malays, Chinese and Indians, respectively. The compromise that was hatched between the coalition partners at the eve of independence failed to fulfil the rising expectations of young generations. The new generation of Malays wanted more and quicker economic gains and the non-Malays (in particular Chinese) were unhappy with the lack of their political control. The resentment culminated in a bloody race riot in May 1969.

The reassessment of earlier compromise following the riot led to the formulation of New Economic Policy (NEP) to be implemented over 20 years to 1990. Its primary objectives were eradication of poverty among all races and of the identification of race with economic function. The latter was designed to give the Malays a greater share in economic wealth with a specific target of raising the share of Malays and other indigenous people (*bumiputra*) to 30 percent of commercial and industrial capital by

1990. It was also recognised that for the maintenance of racial harmony the increase in Malay shares in wealth should not be achieved at the expense of other race. The NEP's role in economic growth with distribution in Malaysia is discussed later.

A new legislation was also introduced immediately after the 1969 riot, which removed such sensitive matters as the powers and status of *Sultans*, Malay special rights, the status of Islam as the official religion and citizen rights from public discussion. Under the leadership of new Prime Minister Tun Abdul Razzak the ruling coalition of UMNO-MCA-MIC was reorganised as Barisan National (National Front) which included other major opposition parties. This was designed to prevent public discussion of sensitive issues which was made seditious, but allowed the bargaining of communal interests to take place in more discrete manner within the government.

As the economic growth rate declined during the early 1980s due to global economic recession, a new element surfaced in Malaysian politics. Intra-racial politics became dominant in the 1980s as coalition partners, especially UMNO and MCA, faced growing discontent among their own constituencies. The Malays, Chinese and Indians became disillusioned and blamed their respective parties in the ruling coalition for not doing enough. This resulted in the formation of new opposition parties by disaffected members who left UMNO or MCA. However, the ruling Alliance managed to fend off opposition attacks and scored victory in successive elections. The resounding victory of BN and its dominant partner UMNO, especially in opposition heartlands, in the 1995 election has strengthened the leadership of Dr. Mahathir against the opposition both within and outside his own party. Dr. Mahathir has further consolidated his position by succeeding in bringing the breakaway faction of Tenku Razaleigh into the UMNO fold, and securing an UMNO ruling that at the triennial party elections in October, 1996 his and the deputy's position will be uncontested. It seems that by having a potential rival in Razaleigh and the provision of no contest, Mahathir has effectively blocked any challenge to his leadership from the more ambitious Deputy Leader Anwar Ibrahim.

The 1980s also witnessed the growing tension between the executive government of Dr. Mahathir who became the Prime Minister in 1981 and the traditional Malay rulers. Dr. Mahathir won public support in his attempt to restrict the powers and privileges of *Sultans* which shows the weaning of traditional values in a modernising society where public tolerance for the excesses of feudal rulers declines. A new code of conduct was agreed in July 1992 with the *Sultans* outlining the parameters of their involvement in both politics and commerce. The constitutional amendments, approved in May 1994, further curbed the powers of *Sultans* by restricting their personal legal immunity. The amendments also introduced a mandatory code of ethics for judges to be drawn up by the government. This has the potential to jeopardise the separation of the judiciary and the executive.

The economy

With the "Vision 2020", Malaysia aspires to reach a developed country status in the year 2020. This section provides a snap-shot of the spectacular transformation of the Malaysian economy since the adoption of NEP in 1971.

Growth and structural change

Table 3.1 presents the basic macroeconomic indicators of the Malaysian economy. The global recession in the early 1980s, and the collapse of the international tin market in 1985 on top of the slump in oil prices were primarily responsible for a decline in GDP by roughly 1 percent. However, Malaysia successfully came out of recession with a real GDP growth of 5.4 percent in 1987. Real GDP grew at about 9 percent in the subsequent four years.

As can be seen from the table, the inflation rate, measured in terms of changes in consumer price index, has been kept in check. After a slight increase in the inflation rate, it has fallen to 3.6 percent. This was largely achieved by cuts in import duties and other statutory charges. But the economy is showing some signs of distress as the inflation rate and the current account deficits are worsening.

The economic growth and the compulsory employee provident fund contributed largely to a rapid rise in savings rate. But t he economic buoyancy and ambitious infrastructure projects have resulted in a sharp rise in current account deficit, which jumped from less than 4 percent of GDP in 1993 to slightly over 9 percent in 1995.

Table 3.2 shows the rapid structural change of the Malaysian economy during the past two decades. Manufacturing which contributed only 16.4 percent to GDP of a predo minantly agricultural and primary producing country, now accounts for 40

Table 3.1
Basic macroeconomic indicators

Indicator	Year			
	1971-1980	1981-1990	1993	1995
Real GDP growth rate (%)	7.8	5.2	8.3	9.6
Inflation rate (%)	6.0	3.2	3.6	4.2
Share in GDP (%)				
Gross domestic saving	29.1	33.0	35.9	36.7
Gross domestic investment	24.9	30.7	35.0	37.6
Current account	-1.2[a]	-1.9[b]	-3.3	-9.2Debt
Servicing ratio (% exports)	4.6[a]	29.0[b]	7.9	5.0

Sources : Agricultural Development Bank, *Outlook,* (various issues).
Notes : a : 1980; b: 1985.

Table 3.2
Sectoral contributions to GDP (%)

Sector	1975	1980	1985	1990	1995
			Year		
Agriculture	27.7	22.9	20.7	18.7	15.9
Industry	26.8	37.0	36.7	38.5	44.7
Manufacturing	16.4	19.8	19.7	26.9	40.0
Mining & quarrying	4.6	10.1	10.5	9.7	10.3
Services	45.5	40.1	42.6	42.8	39.4

Sources: Asian Development Bank, *Key Indicators* (various issues).

percent of the total output in the economy. Manufacturing grew by an average annual rate of 10 percent during the 1970s and 9.4 percent between 1980-1991. The average growth rate of manufacturing was 12-13 percent per annum during 1991-94. On the other hand, agriculture grew by an annual average rate of around 5 and 4 percent in the 1970s and 1980s, respectively.

As can be seen from Table 3.3, most manufacturing activities could hold on to their position in terms of their share in manufacturing value added (MVA) during the 1980s. The big losers, though, were food, beverage and tobacco (ISIC 31), wood and furniture (ISIC 33), and rubber products, whereas chemicals (ISIC 351, 352), electrical machinery (ISIC 383) and transport equipment (ISIC 384) registered gains. Electrical equipment which include television receivers, video cassette recorders, air-conditioners, personal computers, typewriters and domestic refrigeration was the fasted growing activities. Its average annual growth rate of about 19 percent was nearly 10 percentage point higher than the overall growth of the manufacturing sector during 1980-91, resulting in an increase in its share in MVA from 12 percent in 1979 to 22 percent in 1989.

Despite some structural change within the manufacturing sector, it still remains primarily labor-intensive. After rising very rapidly (20.0 percent per annum) during 1980-85, the growth of the capital-labor ratio dropped to -0.2 percent during 1985-91.[3] This temporary growth in the capital-labor ratio was as a result of major restructuring of the electronic industry and the launching of heavy industries. The failure to raise capital-intensity significantly, has serious implications for the labor market as discussed in a subsequent section.

Table 3.3
Share in manufacturing value added (at factor costs %)

Industry	Year			
	1979	1985	1989	Growth rate (%) 1980-91
Food, beverage & tobacco	25	21	13	2.8
TCF & leather products	7	5	6	8.2
Wood prod. & furniture	12	6	7	n.a
Paper & printing	5	5	5	n.a
Chemicals	6	16	11	7.6
Petroleum & coal	4	4	2	8.1
Rubber	10	5	6	5.0
Plastic, pottery, glass & non-metal products	7	9	9	8.9
Iron & non-ferrous metal	6	7	7	8.7
Machinery	3	2	4	n.a
Electrical machinery	12	15	22	18.8
Transport equipment	4	4	6	11.9
Professional equipment	1	1	1	n.a
Other	1	1	1	n.a

Sources : The United Nations, *Yearbook of Industrial Statistics* (various issues).

External trade

The rapid structural change of the Malaysian economy is also reflected in its external trade. Table 3.4 depicts Malaysia's major exports by sectors. The share of agricultural products in total merchandise exports dropped from nearly 44 percent in 1980 to about 13 percent in 1993. Similarly, the importance of petroleum and other mineral products declined sharply from 34 percent in 1980 to about 14 percent in 1993. On the other hand, manufacturing's share in total merchandise exports rose from 22 percent to 74 percent during the same period. Since 1990, manufacturing exports grew on an average by 30 percent per annum.

The composition of manufacturing exports, too, changed significantly. For example, the share of electrical machinery in manufacturing exports dropped from 40 percent in 1980 to 22 percent in 1992. This drop was taken up almost entirely by telecommunications equipment whose share rose from 3 percent to 19 percent. Sound recorders and office machines also increased their share from less than one percent to 7 and 9 percent, respectively during 1980-92.

Malaysia's industrialisation process depends highly on imported capital and intermediate products. Together, they account for nearly 80 percent of Malaysia's imports. The rapid industrialisation and economic growth have been generating

Table 3.4
Major Malaysian exports (% of total export value)

Sector	Year		
	1989	1992	1994[a]
Manufactures	54.7	69.8	78.3
Crude petroleum	11.0	8.7	4.5
Palm oil	6.7	5.2	4.5
Sawn logs	6.3	3.7	1.7
Rubber	6.5	2.2	1.6
Liquefied natural gas	3.0	2.3	1.7
Tin	1.8	0.7	0.4
Other commodities	10.0	7.4	7.3

Source : DFAT, 1995; Notes : a: January-July.

import demands and merchandise imports grew by 36 percent, 30 percent and 26 percent in 1989, 1990 and 1991, respectively. In the first seven months of 1994, imports of investment goods rose by 29 percent and intermediate goods by 35 percent. Total merchandise imports grew by 32 percent in 1994. Table 3.5 presents the composition of Malaysian imports by types of use.

The high dependence of foreign investment for industrialisation and the consequent repatriation of profits and dividends resulted in consistent deficits on services trade. Freight and insurance payments also place a significant strain on the services account. This is offset to some extent by increased international tourism revenues.

Singapore, Japan, the US and European Union are Malaysia's major trading partner. Together they account for more than 65 percent of exports and 70 percent of imports.

Table 3.5
Malaysian imports by types of use (% of total)

Goods category	Year		
	1990	1992	1994
	(Jan. - Aug.)	(Jan. - Dec.)	(Jan. - Jul)
Investment goods	36.4	42.0	40.8
Intermediate goods	41.3	41.3	43.9
Manufacturing goods	31.8	32.1	n.a
Consumption goods	21.5	16.1	14.7
Imports for re-exports	0.8	0.6	0.5

Source : Same as Table 3.4.

The Asian NIEs are also becoming important trading partners. Malaysia's competitiveness, measured in terms of real exchange rate, with Japan has registered a sharp increase in recent times, as yen continues to strengthen. Its competitiveness with East Asia has also been increasing, albeit slowly. But there is a sign of declining competitiveness with industrial countries taken together.

Table 3.6 shows the geographical distribution of Malaysia's exports and imports. The discrepancy in the shares of exports to and imports from Japan and the US is a reflection of the fact that Japan is increasingly using Malaysia as a production platform for labor-intensive and medium-tech products for exports to the US.

Foreign investment

Malaysia's policy of wooing foreign investment through a combination of attractive incentive packages and the provision of infrastructural support in the export processing zones was extremely successful in attracting multinationals. According to the World Bank, Malaysia was one of the top five recipients of foreign direct investment (FDI) in the developing world during 1987-1991.[4] Strong economic growth, political, and macroeconomic stability, availability of trained manpower and

Table 3.6
Malaysia's trading partners (% of total)

Country	Year		
	1989 (Jan. - July)	1992 (Jan. - Dec.)	1994 (Jan. - July)
Singapore	19.2	23.3	20.7
	13.7	15.9	14.4
United States	17.8	18.6	21.2
	16.5	16.9	17.1
Japan	16.5	13.2	12.1
	24.3	25.9	27.0
Other ASEAN	5.8	6.5	6.6
	5.4	4.7	4.6
European Union	14.9	14.8	12.6
	13.7	12.6	12.6
Asian NIEs/China	5.3	3.4	10.4
	4.7	8.0	10.4
Others	20.5	20.2	16.4
	21.7	16.0	13.9

Source : Same as Table 3.4.
Notes : 1st row = exports to; 2nd row = imports from.

good physical infrastructure attracted high levels of much needed foreign investment. Figure 3.1 shows that inflow of foreign direct investment (FDI) increased rapidly since 1989. In response to government policy changes, FDI rebounded in 1994 after a drop in the previous year. In the first nine months of 1994, the Ministry of Trade and Industry approved 457 projects with foreign investment components of M$9.61 million compared with 390 projects worth M$3.23 million in the corresponding period of 1993. In addition to attractive tax incentives, appreciation of yen and merger and acquisition activities of multinational corporations also contributed to the high inflow of foreign capital. However, Malaysia will continue to face competition from other low-wage countries.

Taiwan, Japan, the US, EEC and Singapore are the major sources of FDI into Malaysia. In 1990, Taiwan and Japan accounted for 35.8 percent and 24 percent of FDI, respectively. Taiwan's share in FDI in 1994 stood at 24.1 percent and that of Japan at 20.4 percent. Among the other major sources of FDI, in 1994, the US supplied 11.6 percent, Singapore 9.5 percent and Hong Kong 8.2 percent.

Manufacturing received the bulk of FDI, with concentration in electrical and electrical activities. Chemicals, coal and petroleum products, mechanical equipment and textiles industries also attracted substantial FDI.

Figure 3.1
Foreign direct investment in Malaysia (in billion U.S. $)

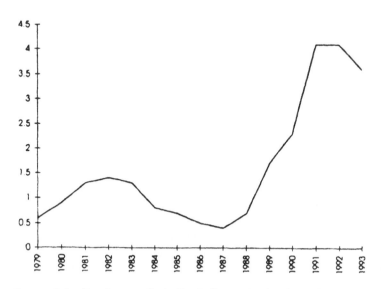

Source: Asian Development Bank, *Key Indicators,*(various issues.)

53

Malaysia is trying to reduce its dependence on multinationals and has a target of 60:40 ratio between domestic and foreign investment. The ratio has increased from 40:60 in 1993 to 46:54 in 1994. In order to accelerate the achievement of the target, the government has set up a M$1 billion domestic investment fund in the 1995 budget. This will be supplemented by an allocation of M$71.6 million to develop basic infrastructure for small and medium sized industries.

In line with the general trend observed in other NIEs, Malaysia is turning into a capital exporting country.[5] In 1990, FDI outflow from Malaysia stood at US$205 million. The major recipients of Malaysian FDI were Papua New Guinea, Singapore, Thailand and the UK. However, recently the aviation industry in the US and the Japanese services sector are attracting Malaysian funds. ASEAN as a whole received 23 percent of Malaysian investment between 1988 and 1993. About 35 companies invested in China and Malaysian investors are concentrating on the regional niche markets, such as Viet Nam and Cambodia, and on raw material-based industries in which they possess management skills.[6] In order to encourage Malaysian overseas investment, a new statutory board, the Malaysia Trade Development Corporation, was set up in 1993 and the 1995 budget has exempted income remitted from abroad fully from tax.

Labor market developments

The continued buoyancy in the economy has resulted in a steady decline of the unemployment rate from the peak of 8.7 percent in 1987 to 2.9 percent in 1994. The market for skilled work force, particularly in manufacturing and construction, is extremely tight. As the boom in manufacturing, services and construction sector draws workers from the traditional sectors, the plantation sector is increasingly becoming dependent on migrant workers. According to the Asian Development Bank estimates, at least half a million of the total labor force of eight million are foreign workers.[7] Another estimate shows that there are about 200,000 illegal foreign workers in Malaysia.[8] According to the Economist, 'at least one million immigrants-- now fill lower-paid jobs. More worrying is the lack of qualified Malaysian staff to fill senior technical and managerial posts'.[9]

The government imposed a ban on further recruitments of foreign workers on January 8, 1994 to allow the police to complete a crackdown on illegal migrants. The heavy-handed dealing by the government has failed to stem the flow of illegal migrant workers. Rather, the trade in migrant workers has gone more underground with serious violations of human rights and rise in labor costs.[10] The ban was lifted in the middle of the 1995 and the manufacturing and construction sectors were allowed to recruit skilled and semi-skilled foreign workers and to hire from the pool of foreign workers already within the country.[11]

Education and training has received the largest ever allocation in 1995 budget as a response to skill shortage. A host of tax incentives are also offered to the private sector for implementing technical or vocational training programs or automation projects. The Human Resource Development Act of 1992 allows firms employing 50 or more Malaysian workers are eligible to apply for government assistance. These firms are required to contribute 1 percent of the their workers' wage to the Human Resource Development Fund (HRDF). Institutions which run approved training programs can also apply for the Industrial Building Allowance. Government has also embarked on privatisation of several education and training institutions.

The tight labor market is fuelling wages growth. The wages in the manufacturing sector grew at a rate of 11-12 percent in 1993 and 1994. The labor productivity growth, on the other hand, lagged behind. According to the Malaysian Institute of Economic Research, the productivity gap is about 6 percent.[12]

The tight labor market has also forced the government to allow female workers in the night shift. The female participation rate in the manufacturing labor force dramatically since 1980, especially in the electronic sector.[13] There has also been a narrowing of male-female wage gap. In some industries (for example, book binding, weaving) the average female monthly earnings exceed that of males.

Malaysia is well-known for a very tough industrial relations legislation. To begin with trade union activities were not allowed in the "pioneer industries" until the early 1970s. The Trade Union Act of 1959 required the unions to confine their membership to employees within a particular trade. Union power was further curtailed in the Industrial Relations Act of 1967 by prohibiting unions to bargain for better terms of employment involving promotions, retrenchments, transfers and allocation of duties.

As a consequence, union's role in Malaysia have been limited to bargaining on limited issues; examples include wages and defending workers on certain basic rights ....[14]

There is no legislated minimum wage in Malaysia. Industrial relations are governed by the Employment Act of 1995 which allows for enterprise bargaining. In response to an increase in industrial accidents, the government has introduced an Occupational Safety and Health Act.

The government discourages the formation of national unions and only about 10 percent of the labor force is unionised. The key private sector unions are the Malaysian Trade Union Congress (MTUC) and the Malaysian Labor Organisation (MLO). The MLO is a splinter group of MTUC and blessed by the government.

Government policies

Malaysian development and the role played by the state owe much to the ethnic 'settlement' that was bargained among the Malays, Chinese and Indians at the time of independence in 1957. The leaders of the three ethnic groups agreed at independence to a modus vivendi: recognition by the Chinese and the Indians of the primacy of Malay political power and of special rights and privileges for Malays, in return for full citizenship rights and a voice in government. This bargain also meant that the Chinese would continue to have economic dominance as long as they did not challenge the political dominance of the Malays.[15] This broad agreement among the three ethnic groups regarding the separation of roles severely limited the state's ability to act autonomously. The laissez faire economic policy in the 1960s can largely be explained in this light. According to Bowie:

> Malay leaders, recognizing that Chinese and Indian political acceptance of UMNO hegemony was conditional on the state's not interfering in private commerce and industry, beyond the performance of its traditional regulatory functions, were constrained from imposing any particular vision of Malaya's industrial future on the private sector. Moreover, all parties to the settlement shared a common interest in suppressing claims to special treatment (i.e., state promotion of particular manufacturing industries over others).[16]

Thus, the communal settlement of 1959 contributed to Malaysia's economic growth in the first decade of her independence in at least three ways. First and most significantly, it ensured that the Chinese economic dynamism was not interrupted. Second, it shielded the state from rent-seeking activities during the import substituting industrialisation phase of the 1960s. Third, it provided the stability which many decolonised nations like India and Pakistan did not enjoy. This made Malaysia attractive to foreign investment at the time when multinationals were looking for off-shore production platforms. It must also be mentioned that being constrained in its policy toward the industrial sector, the government's development efforts during the 1960s focused primarily on the rural-agricultural sector. As a result, rural and agricultural sector received bulk of the public investment. The agricultural and rural development spending accounted for 17.6 percent of public investment during 1961-65 and 26.3 percent during 1966-70 as opposed to 2.5 percent and 3.3 percent for the industrial development during the corresponding periods.[17] The focus on rural and agricultural sector also matched with UMNO's concern to establish its legitimacy with the Malay population, majority of whom lived in rural areas. The heavy infrastructural development in rural areas contributed significantly to the growth of agricultural output.

The race riot of 1969 and the New Economic Policy (NEP)

Although the laissez faire approach to commerce and industry was found to be congenial to economic growth as it ensured the Chinese economic dynamism, it perpetuated "separate and unequal" development of the three ethnic communities. As expected most of the benefits of economic growth was raked in by the Chinese community. This widened the gap between the Malays and Chinese. The small number of new generation Malay entrepreneurs felt the Chinese competitive edge and began to question the validity of the 1957 bargain. At the same time, the non-Malays were resentful of Malay "special rights" and felt a keen sense of discrimination.[18] The growing ethnic tension culminated in the violent race riot of May 13, 1969.

The events of 1969 represent a major watershed in Malaysia's economic and political history. As mentioned earlier, politically, the riot meant an end of the earlier communal settlement on the separation of economic and political roles along ethnic lines. In economic terms, it ended the laissez faire approach to commerce and industry. The Malay political leadership responded to the riot with the New Economic Policy (NEP) which provided the state with the vehicle for a more active role in economic affairs.

The primary thrust of the NEP was to 'accelerate the process of restructuring Malaysian society to correct economic imbalance, so as to reduce and eventually eliminate the identification of race with economic function'.[19] The state became the main instrument for this economic reorganisation. With a view to increasing the Malay share in business and employment a large number of state corporations were set up along with the introduction of quotas on enrolments for different ethnic groups in public educational institutions. Government also used preferential credit system to channel funds to Malay business and to preferred industrial sectors.

NEP : a recipe for disaster?

According to the neo-classical political economy, the above expanded role of the state as proclaimed in the NEP is a recipe for disaster as it distorts the price signals. In addition, the interventionist state becomes a fertile ground for rent-seeking and directly unproductive activities by vested interest groups, which in this case is clearly the Malay ethnic community. One can, in fact, cite numerous examples where state interventions went wrong. According to Balassa[20], over a half of state enterprises posted loss in 1986. Among them is the most notorious example of M$2.5 billion loss by *bumiputra* Malaysia Finance which revealed the corruption and personal interests of the management.[21] Government's heavy industries initiatives of the early 1980s were also largely regarded as disappointing.[22] In particular, the rapid growth of public enterprises such as Heavy Industries Corporation of Malaysia (HICOM) resulted in the "crowding out" of private sector industry. These public enterprises have enjoyed preferential access to finance and the government has not allowed private industries to compete freely with state enterprises. The public corporations have also enjoyed advantages in procuring government contracts.[23]

NEP's education policy and push for Malay human resource development has also been responsible for graduate unemployment. For example, a survey in 1983 found that some six months after graduation 35.5 percent of graduates who were on government scholarships were still unemployed.[24] Yet the bonded nature of scholarships prevented them from seeking jobs in the private sector. The distortion in the allocation of skilled human resources is also reflected from the fact that more that 80 percent graduates work for the government and statutory bodies.

There were also macro level distortions. For example, with the NEP, the budget deficit increased by 120 percent from M$476 million in 1970 to M$1.0 billion in 1971. Between 1979 and 1981 the Malaysian government had to rely heavily on deficit budgets to sustain NEP's high economic growth targets in the face of adverse international economic trends. It could not deviate from its course of high public investment in favor of Malays.[25] As a result, the federal government debt as a proportion of GNP rose from 10 percent in 1980 to 30 percent in 1985.

Malaysia's external debt, too, increased quite alarmingly. In 1983, the total external debt as proportion of GNP was 49 percent, well above the developing country average of 36 percent. The public external debt in the same year was 39 percent of GNP. The external debt rose to 56 percent in 1985.[26]

Nevertheless, the Malaysian economy grew remarkably during the past two decades (except for during the mid-1980s). It is poised to graduate into a newly industrialising economy. What role did the NEP play in the transformation of the Malaysian economy? Can we regard the NEP as a recipe for disaster?

NEP : a formula for growth with distribution

Although the NEP changed the nature of inter-communal settlement, in the core of it was the objective of maintaining national unity and political stability. In the words of one of the architects of the NEP, the present Prime Minister, Dr. Mahathir Mohammad:

> [the NEPs] formulation was made necessary by the economic needs of the nation as much as its politico-social needs. There can be no economic stability without political stability and social stability. Thus the NEP is also a formula for economic growth.[27]

Therefore, the most important catalyst role the NEP played in the economic growth of Malaysia is the provision of social and political stability. The NEP proclaimed the uplifting of Malay fortunes as one of the fundamental pre-requisites for social stability. It was argued that a more equitable distribution of wealth and a more balanced participation of all ethnic communities in the modern sector of the economy is 'a sine qua non, an indispensable condition for a united Malaysian nation in the longer run and an essential requisite for political survival and stability in the shorter term'.[28]

It was also realised by the Malay political leadership that while short-term political and social stability can be achieved through redistribution of wealth and appeasing the Malays, a zero-sum distributional policy would mean longer-term disaster. Thus, the redistribution of wealth was perceived within a growing economy. As stated in the Second Malaysia Plan, 1971-75 (p. 1):

> The New Economic Policy is based upon a rapidly expanding economy which offers increasing opportunities for all Malaysians as well as additional resources for development. Thus, in the implementation of this policy, the Government will ensure that no particular group will experience loss or feel any sense of deprivation. (Emphasis added).

Thus, the NEP represented a Pareto optimal solution to social and economic problems in so far as the distributional objective was pursued within the context of an expanding pie. It became almost imperative for the Malay dominated government to pursue growth-oriented policies if it were to maintain racial harmony and draw support from all Malaysians. Thus, although the Malaysian state is captured by one particular ethnic community, the ethnic imperatives curtailed the state's ability to pursue narrow distributional objectives at the cost of long-term growth. This conclusion is in sharp contrast with Bowie's pessimistic view of the Malaysian state that 'in fragmented societies, short-run policies favoring wealth redistribution will take precedence over policies promoting long-run economic growth.'[29]

The NEP's explicit objective of wealth redistribution within a growing economy continued to dominate Malaysia's five year plans. For example, the Third Malaysia Plan, 1976-80 (1976: 7) was formulated:

> to eradicate poverty among all Malaysians and to restructure Malaysian society so that the identification of race with economic function and geographic location is reduced and eventually limited, both objectives being realised through the rapid expansion of the economy over time. (Emphasis added).

Malaysian Industrial Policy Studies (MIPS)
and Industrial Master Plan (IMP)

As the completion year of NEP drew nearer, the government commissioned two studies to evaluate the achievements of NEP and formulate policies to ensure that NEP targets are met. The first is the Malaysian Industrial Policy Studies (MIPS) and the second, Industrial Master Plan (IMP) covering the period 1986-95. The MIPS examined tax and tariff incentives for industrialisation and recommended reductions in the rate of protection. The IMP emphasised 12 key industries and gave details of how linkages and diversification of the manufacturing base could be achieved.

Following the recommendations of IMP, the government introduced a series of legislation to encourage foreign investment. These included the relaxation of foreign equity rules in 1986, the freeing of credit restrictions in 1987 and the withdrawal of proposals to abandon tax incentives for foreign firms. The government also introduced the New Investment Fund in 1985 and the Industrial Adjustment Fund in 1987 to encourage domestic private investment.

New Development Policy (NDP) and recent policy developments

In June 1991, the government announced the New Development Policy (NDP) to succeed NEP. The NDP replaced the racially based economic and social policy with national unity. Although the 30 percent target for *bumiputra* corporate ownership was retained, no specific deadline was set for its achievement. It was regarded that the shortage of Malays with relevant management and technical qualifications was an impediment to the achievement of *bumiputra* ownership target. Thus, the NDP emphasises human resource development as is reflected in the Six Malaysian Plan (1991-95). The Seventh Malaysian Plan (1996-00) will continue to place strong emphasis on technical and vocational skills training and investment in R & D capabilities in order to reduce dependence on foreign investment and technology.

As a means of reducing the dependence of multinationals, the NDP targeted the development of small and medium sized industries (SMI). The Domestic Investment Initiative (DII) has been launched with a view to encouraging domestic value-added production, strengthening SMIs and improving the accessibility of the local capital market.

The NDP forms the basis of the Prime Minister Dr. Mahathir's 'Vision 2020', the date by which he intended Malaysia to attain a developed country status. The NDP's macroeconomic and social targets are contained in the Outline Perspective Plan for 1991-00. According to the Outline Perspective Plan, the real GDP is projected to grow at an average annual rate of 7 percent and the share of manufacturing in exports is projected to increase to more than 80 percent.

Although the Malaysian government is very proactive in its industrial and economic policy, close cooperation between the government and the private sector is an important aspect of the NDP's economic policy agenda. It envisages that the private sector in the new era will play more leading role. Thus, the government has one of the most comprehensive and broad-ranging privatisation programs in the region.[30] The government has privatised 103 entities by May 1994 and over 15 previously government-owned companies which include the national energy company, Tenaga Nasional, Heavy Industries Corporation of Malaysia (HICOM) and Telekom, have been listed on the Kuala Lumpur Stock Exchange. Under the Rolling Action Privatisation Plan 1994/95, 78 projects have been identified for privatisation, followed by 77 projects in 1995. The 1994 program includes the development of seaports in Penang, Johor and Kelang, the commissioning of independent power producers and the development of a new television station. Aspects of the new Kuala Lumpur International Airport, the ports of Kuantan and Kemaman, the National Savings Bank and the housing loan division of the Ministry of Finance are earmarked for privatisation in 1995.

The foreign companies are allowed to participate in these projects provided relevant local expertise is not available, local capital is insufficient and the participation is necessary for export promotion. Foreign equity is, however, restricted to 25 percent of share capital.

Export-oriented industrialisation remains the main vehicle for achieving the "Vision 2020". The government policy is encouraging core dynamic industries that are capable of competing internationally without significant protection. Thus, the government has embarked on ambitious trade liberalisation program. In 1994, tariff duties on 600 items have been cut and the 1995 budget targets over 2,600 products, most of them food and consumer goods, for tariff reductions. However, the agricultural sector as a whole and some key manufacturing activities such as automobiles, paper and plastic resins and a range of processed agricultural products continue to receive high protection. There is also limited protection for some key service sector activities.

Although the government desires to reduce the dependence on foreign investment and achieve a 60:40 ratio between domestic investment and FDI, it still actively seeks FDI. In order to remain competitive with emerging low cost countries in Indochina, and China, the Malaysian government in October 1993 introduced attractive incentive packages which included reductions in corporate taxes and import duties on a wide ranging items.

Concluding remarks

To the extent labor was repressed and the government pursued a "directive" industrial policy, the remarkable transformation of Malaysia fits the conventional "statist" paradigm. But authoritarian feature of the "strong state" derived from Confucian ethics certainly does not apply to ethnically diverse Malaysia. The state is also not autonomous as it follows explicit pro-bumiputra policies, and is not free from rent-seeking as various corruption candles show. The durability of Malaysian success also defies neo-classical explanation which regards active sector specific government interventions in the economy as a recipe for disaster. This paper has argued that the rapid transformation of the Malaysian economy lies in its desire to maintain racial harmony within the context of an expanding economy. Thus, the policy makers never traded off growth for redistributive objectives.

Malaysian economy has reached a critical juncture in its march toward becoming a fully developed country. In the short-run, while it has to deal with labor shortage in general, in the longer-run it must move to restructuring its manufacturing toward skill and capital intensive activities. The question is : will the present system serve Malaysia equally in its move to an "innovation driven" society? There is a growing body of literature which shows that innovation thrives most in an open political system, where the state plays only a supportive role (Chowdhury and Islam, 1993). Thus, how Malaysia handles the growing desire of its citizens for a more open and plural democracy will determine the success in its next phase of transformation.

Notes

1   This chapter is based on author's book, Islam and Chowdhury, 1996.

2   This section draws heavily on Brown, 1996.

3   Rasiah, 1995, p. 84.

4   DFAT, 195, p.15.

5   OECD, 1993.

6   ADB, 1994, p. 107.

7   ADB, ibid. p. 103.

8   APEG, 1994, p. 150.

9   *The Economist*, May 11, 1996, p. 26.

10   *Far Eastern Economic Review*, May 23, 1996.

11   ADB, op cit. p. 104.

12   DFAT, op cit. p. 32.

13   Rasiah, op cit. p. 87.

14   Rasiah, ibid. pp. 77-78.

15   Bowie, 1988, p. 54; Alamgir, 1994, p. 70.

16   Bowie, 1991, p. 74.

17   Bowie, ibid. p. 69.

18   Sivalingam, 1998, p. 39.

19   *Second Malaysia Plan*, 1971-75, p. 1.

20   Balassa, 1991, p. 148.

21   Bowie, 1988, p. 64.

22   UNDP/World Bank, 1985; MIDA/UNIDO, 1985.

23 Bowie, 1988, p. 63.

24 Mehmet, 1987, p. 89.

25 Alamgir, op cit, p. 73.

26 See Jomo, 1987, pp 124-130.

27 Mahathir, 1976, p. 9.

28 Musa, 1986, p. 6.

29 Bowie, 1988, p. 53.

30 DFAT, op cit. p. 16

References

Asian Development Bank (ADB), *Asian Development Outlook,* 1994, Manila: ADB, 1994.

Asia Pacific Economic Group (APEG), *Asia Pacific Profiles,* 1994, Canberra: Australian National University, 1994.

Brown, I. 'Malaysia - History', *The Far East and Australasia 1996,* 26th ed., Europa Publications Ltd., 1996.

Alamgir, J., "Formula and Fortune : Economic Development in Malaysia", *Journal of Contemporary Asia,* Vol. 24, No. 1: 67-80, 1994.

Balassa, B., *Economic Policies in the Pacific Area Developing Countries,* New York: New York University Press, 1991.

Bowie, A., "Redistribution with Growth? The Dilemmas of State Sponsored Development in Malaysia", in Clark, C. and Lemaco, J. (eds.) *State and Development,* Leiden : E.J. Brill, 1988.

Bowie, A., *Crossing the Industrial Divide: State, Society and the Policies of Economic Transformation in Malaysia,* New York: Columbia University Press, 1991.

Chowdhury, A. and Islam, I., *The Newly Industrialising Economies of East Asia,* London & NY : Routledge, 1993.

Department of Foreign Affairs and Trade (DFAT), *Malaysia - Country Brief,* Canberra: Government of Australia, 1995.

The Economist, 'Malaysia : Grand Plans', May 11: 26, 1996.

The Far Eastern Economic Review, 1996, 'Labor : Vital and Vulnerable', May vol. 23, no. 60-67, 1996.

Government of Malaysia, *Second Malaysia Plan,* 1971-75, Kuala Lumpur: Government Printer, 1971.

Government of Malaysia, *Third Malaysia Plan,* 1976-80, Kuala Lumpur: Government Printer, 1976.

Government of Malaysia, *Fourth Malaysia Plan*, 1981-85, Kuala Lumpur: Government Printer, 1981.

Islam, I. and Chowdhury, A., *The Asia-Pacific Economies*, London & NY: Routledge, 1996.

Jomo, K.S., "Economic Crisis and Policy Response in Malaysia", in Robinson, R., Hewison, K. and Higgott, R. (eds.) *Southeast Asia in the 1980s: The Politics of Economic Crisis*, London: Allen & Unwin, 1987.

Mahathir bin Mohammad, "Speech by Y.A.B. Dr. Mahathir Mohammad, Deputy Prime Minister/Education Minister", delivered at the opening of the *Federation of Malaysian Manufacturers Seminar on the Third Malaysian Plan*, Kuala Lumpur, August 26, 1976.

Mehmet, O., "The Malaysian Experience in Manpower Planning and Labor Market Policies", in Amjad, R. (ed.), *Human Resource Planning : The Asian Experience*, New Delhi: ILO-ARTEP, 1987.

MIDA/UNDP, *Medium and Long Term Industrial Master Plan Malaysia 1986-95*, Kuala Lumpur : Government Printer, 1985.

Musa, H., "Keynote Address" delivered at the *Conference on Malaysia*, Tufts University, Medford, Mass. Nov. 18-20, 1986.

OECD, *Foreign Direct Investment Relations Between the OECD and the Dynamic Asian Economies*, Paris: OECD, 1993.

Rasiah, R., 'Labor and Industrialization', *Journal of Contemporary Asia*, vo.25, no. 1, 73-92, 1995.

Sivalingam, G., "The New Economic Policy and the Differential Economic Performance of the Races in West Malaysia, 1970-85", in Nash, M. (ed.) *Economic Performance in Malaysia: The Insider's View*, New York: Professors World Peace Academy, 1988.

UNDP/World Bank *Final Report: Malaysian Industrial Policy Studies Project*, Kuala Lumpur: Government Printer, 1985.

4 Economic development in the Philippines: a frustrated take-off?

Mahabub Hossain [1]
International Rice Research Institute

Abstract

Since the early 1980s the Philippine economy has been suffering from a serious setback.It has been plagued with a prolonged recession accompanied by political unrest including separatist movement. In order to solve these multiple problems, international development agencies recommended standard policy prescriptions. But politically strong vested interest group did not let the Philippine government implement these policies wholeheartedly. As a result, attempts to end economic recession had failed. This chapter explains the resource base and development challenges facing the Philippine economy today. It also outlines appropriate policies and strategies to meet those challenges and records progress made in the various sectors of the economy. In the light of the present trend, the chapter highlights the future prospects of the Philippine economy.

Introduction

The Philippines was one of the progressive nations in Asia in the early 1950s. During three decades after the Second World War, its economic performance was no less remarkable than other Southeast Asian nations. But a prolonged economic recession since early 1980s, when the neighboring countries have accelerated their economic growth, has turned the Philippines into a "sick man of Asia." The recent development history of this country is characterized by political conflicts including a separatist insurgency in the south, frequent natural disasters including the eruption of Mount Pinatubo in 1991, consistently high inflation, a chronic external debt overhang, repressed financial system, regressive taxation, dilapidated economic infrastructure, sluggish and erratic economic growth, and a highly skewed income distribution which is epitomized by a huge disparity in urban and rural living conditions. Multilateral development agencies have pushed standard prescription to remedy the economic ills, which faced stiff resistance from politically strong vested interest groups, and the government has made only half-hearted attempts to implement them. After three years of relatively strong political leadership since 1992, there is a ray of hope that economic recession in the Philippines may soon be over.

The present chapter explains the resource base and development challenges faced by the economy, outlines policies and strategies pursued to meet those challenges, and records progress made in various sectors of the economy and its impact on the level of living of the people. It concludes by evaluating the prospect of economic recovery in the light of the most recent changes in policies and development trends.

The Philippine's resource base

Natural resource

The Philippines is not as blessed with natural resources as many of its Southeast Asian neighbors. The country has limited reserves of copper, gold, and nickel, which have been seriously depleted from 10.8 billion tons in 1973 to only 3.6 billion tons in 1991. The value added from mining declined from 2.8 percent of the gross national product (GNP) in the early seventies to 1.1 percent in recent years. The Philippines has to import fuel to meet its energy needs; petroleum products accounted for a quarter of its import bills during periods of high economic growth. The economy has been subjected to severe pressures from the oil crisis of the early and late 1970s and during the Gulf War.

Land is an important means of livelihood for the majority of the people but has been under pressure of over exploitation from a growing population and limited employment opportunities in the non-farm sectors. About one-third of the 30 million hectare of land mass of the country is now cultivated with an estimated 4.6 million farm households. The average size of farm is estimated at 2.16 hectare by the agricultural census in 1991, and land available per head of agricultural worker is only 0.94 hectare. The number of farm households increased by 96 percent during the 1971-91 period, which led to an extension of cultivation to village commons and forest margins. During 1971-91, the area under temporary crops grown on lowland valleys increased by 37 percent, while the area under permanent crops grown on highlands and hill slopes increased by 63 percent, seriously depleting the forest reserves.[2]

The village woodlands, fallows, and pastures declined from 2.07 million hectare in 1971 to 0.47 million hectare in 1991. Concerned with the over exploitation of forest resources, the government has converted the unclassified forest land, which comprised 29 percent of the land mass in 1971, to classified forests that now account for almost half of the land area. The government's policy of preserving the forest land has led to a decline in agricultural incomes and export earnings from forest resources. The value added from forestry declined from 3.9 percent of the GNP in 1970 to only 0.38 percent in 1993.

Human resource

In 1995, the Philippines has 68.4 million people within a land area of 300,000 kilometer square, making it one of the most densely populated countries in Southeast Asia. Population density in 1990 was 208 persons per kilometer square of land area, compared with 216 in Vietnam, 110 in Thailand, 100 in Indonesia, 64 in Myanmar, 54 in Malaysia, and 47 in Cambodia. The population is currently growing at 2.2 percent per year, adding 1.5 million people every year. The population is projected to grow another 43 percent within the next 25 years.

A distinguishing characteristic of the Philippines compared with its Southeast Asian neighbors is the quality of its human resources. The mean years of schooling for population aged 25 years or more is 8.0 years for male and 7.2 years for female, one of the highest among the developing world and almost double the level achieved in Thailand. Nearly three quarters of the relevant age group enrol in secondary schools compared with 32 percent in Thailand, 43 percent in Indonesia, and 58 percent in Malaysia. The enrollment ratio at the tertiary level is 27 percent of the age group. The male-female disparity in education is nonexistent in the Philippines. In fact at the secondary and tertiary level, the enrollment ratio is higher for females than for males. The high quality of human resources places the Philippines in a very favorable position in the international labor market. Remittances from overseas workers is an important source of foreign exchange earnings for the country.

Because of the high fertility rate, almost 40 percent of the population are young children, or of school-going age, i.e. below 15 years. Another 5.2 percent of the population are aged 60 or more. Thus, the economically active age group constitutes only 55 percent of the total population, of which nearly 73 percent participate in the labor market. The high participation rate is mainly due to extraordinarily high participation of women in economic activities. The labor force participation rate among the economically active age group is about 92 percent for men and 54 percent for women. Women are more heavily involved in personal and social services and in trade and commerce than men, and they participate almost equally in manufacturing industries. Agriculture, transport, and construction activities employ mostly male workers as depicted in Table 4.1.

Agriculture employs only 45 percent of all workers, compared with more than 60 percent in neighboring countries. By international standards, the growth of labor force is very high. The labor force participation rate rose in 1970 due to increasing female participation. The growth in labor force was 3.4 percent per year during 1971-75, 4.2 percent during 1976-86, and 3.0 percent during 1986-92.

Table 4.1
Utilization of human resources: the occupational
distribution of the labor force.

Occupation	1985(third quarter)			1992(first quarter)			Percent of total labor force in occupation	
	Male	Female	Total	Male	Female	Total	1985	1992
Agriculture	7233	2465	9698	7998	2587	10585	43.8	41.1
Manufacturing and mining	1113	927	2040	1479	1179	2656	9.2	10.3
Economic Infrastructure	737	26	763	1139	35	1174	3.4	4.6
Transport services	889	42	931	1134	55	1189	4.2	4.6
Trade and commerce	1092	1862	2954	1341	2348	3689	13.3	14.3
Personal and social services	1446	1962	3408	1887	2307	4194	15.4	16.3
Unemployed	1473	889	2362	1290	977	2267	10.7	8.8
Total labor force	13983	8173	22156	16268	9488	25754	100	100
Economically active population	15096	15080	30176	17754	17725	35470	–	–

Source: National Statistical Coordination Board, *Philippine Statistical Yearbook*, 1994, Makati, The Philippines.

Development challenges

A formidable development problem for the Philippines is its large population in relation to the natural resources and the relatively rapid growth. Because of the high concentration of assets and economic power in a few hands, it is expected that the economic gains will be unequally distributed. To make a significant dent in the poverty situation, the Philippines has to target a high rate of growth of per capita incomes so that some benefits reach the poor people through the normal market mechanism. If the Philippines wants its per capita income to double every 10 years, the gross national product must increase at 9 percent per year if the population increases annually at 2.0 percent per year. This is the GNP growth target that has been set for the terminal year in the 1993-98 Medium-term Philippine Development Plan.

With the present structure of investment in the economy, the incremental capital/output ratio is estimated at 3.5:1, which will be higher if emphasis were given on infrastructure development and on the growth of manufacturing industries that are

68

more capital-intensive in nature. This means that to attain a 9 percent annual growth, the Philippines must invest at least 32 percent of its GNP for development purposes. Capital accumulation of this magnitude is difficult without substantial inflow of external resources including private foreign investment. A large population impedes private savings as even economically poor households desire to provide at least secondary level education to all children and potential savings are utilized for meeting educational expenses. Since 45 percent of the population are children, the high population growth impedes the government capacity to invest in basic economic infrastructure after providing adequate public funds for human resource development-- i.e, building and maintaining social infrastructures for health, education, and training.

The most formidable challenge to the economy is how to generate productive employment for the labor force currently growing at 3.0 percent per year and how to sustain a growth in labor productivity at rates that provide incentives to employers and increase wage rates on a regular basis. Agriculture is the largest employer, but since agricultural growth will depend on technological progress, the employment generation potential of the sector is severely limited. Also, since most of people are literate, they dislike manual work and there are evidences of premature adoption of agricultural technologies that save manual labor. Additional employment must be generated in the manufacturing and services sector which needs support from the government in terms of massive investment in the development and maintenance of transport and communication infrastructure, and generation and distribution of electric power.

Structure and growth of the economy

Long-term growth

Since 1950, the national income increased at 4.5 percent a year. Much of this growth was offset by the population increase of 2.8 percent per year during the 1950-93 period. Thus, per capita income increased by a meager less than 2 percent per year. This long-term near stagnation of the economy obscures respectable economic progress during the period in question.

Although the Philippine economy was growing slowly, by 1980, it reached a per capita income level of US$929--almost similar to that of Thailand and 40 percent higher than that of Indonesia.[3] In the early 1980s, an economic recession set in from which the country is yet to recover. The GNP growth slowed down to the level of population growth during the 1980-83 period, but then had a large absolute decline after the assassination of Benigno Aquino, the political opponent of President Marcos. This event led to a serious political crisis and ultimately to the downfall of the Marcos Regime through "people's power" in 1986. The GNP dropped by 12 percent and the per capita income by 18 percent during the 1983-86 period. Since then production growth has barely kept pace with population growth. Per capita income in 1993 was still 9 percent lower than the level reached in 1980.

The performance of different sectors of the economy can be reviewed from Table 4.2. The productive sectors, agriculture and industry grew at respectable rates of 4.6 percent and 8.2 percent per year, respectively, during the 1950-80, and the share of manufacturing industry in GNP reached 28 percent by 1980. Most notable was the expansion of economic infrastructure as evidenced by a 14 percent per year growth in value added in construction and power, whose share in GNP increased from 4.4 percent in 1970 to 10.9 percent by 1980. It is the infrastructure and the manufacturing sectors that suffered most during the period of economic recession. The value added in construction activities declined by 60 percent during the 1983-86 period. In the manufacturing industry growth was a meager 0.6 percent per year. Only the services sector, i.e., transport, trade and public administration maintained a modest rate of growth during this long economic recession.

Agriculture

Agriculture accounts for nearly 22 percent of the GDP composed of staple grains rice and corn (5.1 percent); vegetables and fruits (5.2 percent); plantation crops, coconut and banana (1.9 percent); sugarcane (0.7 percent); livestock (4.5 percent); fishery (3.9 percent); and forestry (0.4 percent). Forestry accounted for nearly 3.9 percent of the

Table 4.2
Progress of different economic sectors 1950-93

Sector	Sectoral shares of GDP			Rate of growth (percent/yr)		
	1970	1980	1993	1950-70	1970-80	1980-93
Agriculture	28.2	25.3	21.1	4.6	4.9	1.2
Manufacturing and mining	25.8	28.1	24.3	8.7	7.1	0.6
Construction and power	4.4	10.9	7.7	2.2	14.2	-1.3
Transport and communication	4.3	4.7	5.2	6.9	8.9	3.0
Trade and finance	25.2	21.4	24.1	5.5	4.6	2.4
Other services	13.9	10.2	14.7	6.4	5.1	3.6
Gross domestic product	101.7	100.6	97.2	5.4	6.2	1.4
Gross national product	100.0	100.6	100.0	5.4	6.4	1.7

Source: National Statistics Coordination Board; *Philippine Statistical Yearbook*, various issues.

GDP in 1970, but the government's policy of preservation of forest resources has led to a drastic decline in value added from forestry at 3.5 percent per year during the 1970s, and 13 percent per year since 1980. The deceleration of agricultural growth from 4.8 percent during the 1970s to 1.1 percent during the 1980-93 period was largely due to the contraction of economic exploitation of forest resources.

The period of economic recession also experienced an absolute decline in value added from plantation crops, which performed remarkably well in the 1970s. Value added in coconut plantation, which occupies 26 percent of the cropped land, increased at 5.3 percent during the 1970s, but declined to a negative 4.3 percent during the 1980-93 period. Income from banana plantation had an absolute decline of 2.5 percent per year during 1980-93, compared with an impressive 12.4 percent per year growth during the earlier decade. For sugar, falling world prices, deterioration of the peace and order condition in Negroes Island--the country's sugar bowl, and termination in the mid-1970s of the Laurel-Langley Agreement which provided Philippine sugar exporter access to the lucrative US sugar market under a quota system contributed to its sharp contraction in the 1980s.

The growth of the main staple grain -- rice also contracted from 4.1 percent per year in the 1970s to 2.1 percent in 1980-93. The factors causing the slowdown in production included stagnation of public investment in irrigation, exhaustion of productivity potential of high-yielding modern varieties, diversion of land to nonagricultural uses particularly near urban centers, continued decline in world rice prices, and degradation of crop production environment owing partly to the practice of intensive rice monoculture in irrigated areas and to soil erosion induced by rapid deforestation[4].

The economic recession, however, did not prevent the poultry and livestock sector from sustaining its respectable rate of growth. Livestock and fisheries registered the highest rate of growth 4.8 and 6.1 percent per year, respectively among the various subsectors in agriculture, and was the main driving force behind the growth of agriculture during the 1980-93 period.

Industry

The manufacturing industry accounted for 24 percent of the GDP in 1993, composed mainly of food manufactures (9.6 percent), petroleum products (2.3 percent), chemical products (2.0 percent), garments and footwear (1.7 percent), beverage industry (1.1 percent) and electrical machinery. Surprisingly, textile manufacturing, which is usually an important economic activity in the early stages of development, is of little importance in the Philippine economy. The growth in the manufacturing sector decelerated from 7.0 percent in the 1970s to only 0.6 percent during the 1980-93 period.

In the past, industrialization in the Philippines has been biased strongly toward urban centers through policy-induced import substitution. A basic reason behind the underdeveloped rural industry is the dual structure of the Philippino society, reflecting the highly skewed and unequal distribution which has its origin from the Spanish colonial rule. The opening of the Philippines to the world economy at the turn of this century under the American colonial regime led to rapid economic development based mainly on the expansion of export-oriented plantation crops, coconut, and sugarcane controlled by the absentee large landowners at the expense of household industries in rural areas due to the lack of both effective demand and the investible surplus[5]. As agricultural surpluses are being extracted by landlords, little funds are left in rural areas to be mobilized for investment in rural industries. Partly because of its strong urban bias, the industry sector was hit hardest during the political crisis in the early 1980s. Although the sector has been recovering from the bottom reached in 1985, many manufacturing subsectors have not come back to the production level attained in 1980[6]. The subsectors that registered negative growth during the 1980-93 period are textiles (-2.5 percent per year), food manufacture (-1.1 percent), and chemical products (-0.6 percent). Tobacco manufacturers and nonmetallic materials maintained the status quo. Only electrical machinery and equipment (6.9 percent), petroleum products (5.3 percent), and the beverage industry (4.3 percent) had a moderate rate of growth during the 1980-93 period.

In recent years, the export sector received considerable boost from the rapid expansion of exports of garments and electronic products. The exports of garments also generated considerable employment in rural areas as the business is organized by subcontracting production activities in a large number of small-scale rural enterprises. The number of garment exporters increased from 706 to 1428 during the 1984-93 period, while employment in garment increased by 63 percent. In Laguna Province in Southern Luzon, two-thirds of the subcontracting farms operate with a size of less than 20 workers per unit[7]. The expansion of these two export items did not contribute much to the growth in the industry sector because of low value added ratio.

Infrastructure

In the Philippines, public investment for infrastructure was drastically reduced during the period of political disturbance in early 1980s which contributed to the prolongation of economic recession. It was already high at 5.4 percent of GNP in 1975 and further increased to 6.4 percent of GNP by 1982. This was an important factor behind the vibrant construction activities in the 1970s that provided fuel to the rapid growth in both the agriculture and the manufacturing sectors. During the 1983-85 period, however, public sector investment on physical infrastructure drastically dropped to only 2.8 percent of the GDP; it remained at that level until 1993. The impact of this reduced public spending on expansion of various infrastructure facilities is shown in Table 4.3.

The Philippines suffers from serious shortages of electric power. But electric energy was one of the fastest growing sectors in the 1970s, when production capacity

Table 4.3
Development of physical infrastructure 1970-93

Infrastructure	Year				
	1970	1980	1993	1970-80	1980
Production of energy	6794	18583	26592	10.6	2.8
(million kilowatt hours)					
Length of paved road	4.8	9.3	8.8	6.8	-0.4
(km/100 km² area)					
Length of bridges	163	221	248	3.1	0.9
(000 meter)					
Irrigated area	450	649	785	3.7	1.5
(000 hectare)					

Source: National Statistics Coordination Board; *Philippine Statistical Yearbook*, various issues.

increased at 10.6 percent per year. But growth was drastically reduced to only 2.8 percent per year during 1 980-93. As a result, by late 1980s, the power supply became inadequate in relation to the country's demands. Shortages leading to frequent power failures became a common phenomenon in both rural and urban areas. This led to underutilization of industrial capacity. Many industrial enterprises had to invest in electric generators which increased the cost of production and reduced competitiveness in both international and domestic markets.

The Philippines has an extensive road system but the quality of roads, in general, is poor. The total road density is about 53 kilometer per 100 kilometer square of land area, compared with 17 in Thailand and 12 in Malaysia. But the paved roads constitute only 14 percent of the total road length in the Philippines, compared with 48 percent in Thailand and 80 percent in Malaysia. The better-quality roads are found along the coast which basically serves to connect the water transport which suffers from inadequate port facilities. The interior areas are served mostly by gravel and earth roads which are not available for motorized transports during the long wet season. Because of the poor quality of roads, the unit cost of transport is high, and farmers have to sell their produce immediately after harvest to agents of marketing oligarchy at prices much lower than that prevailing in urban markets.

The length of paved roads increased at an impressive rate of 6.8 percent per year during the 1970s but had an absolute decline since 1984 because of inadequate investment on maintenance. The number of motor vehicles however increased 2.5 times and the number of trucks and utility vans increased 3.6 times during the 1980-93 period, putting extremely high pressure on the stagnant road network, causing traffic jams and wastage of time. Similar was the story for irrigation infrastructure. The facilities built during the 1960s and 1970s could not be properly maintained. There was very little public investment since the early 1980s for generation of new capacity. As a result, growth in irrigated area decelerated from 3.7 percent per year during the 1970s to 1.5 percent in 1980-93. The recent expansion was partly due to private investment on pumps and tubewells.

The quality of irrigation from public systems has deteriorated due to siltation of dams and inadequate maintenance of canals. Many irrigation systems now serve to provide supplementary irrigation during the wet season but fail to provide adequate water to grow rice during the dry season. In important constraint to expansion of public investment on infrastructure is the underpricing of the services and the government's failure to recoup the initial investment from the users. In recent years, the government has been encouraging private sector investment in infrastructure activities.

External trade

Foreign trade accounts for a large segment of the Philippine economy, but for most of the years since the early 1970s the Philippines suffered huge deficits in the balance of trade. In 1993, export earnings accounted for 20.5 percent and import payments 33.8 percent of the GDP. The changes in the composition of the export and import trade can be reviewed from Table 4.4.

Traditional export items are copper concentrates, copra, coconut oil, centrifugal and refined sugar, logs and lumber, and abaca products. Except for coconut products, most of these items experienced a downward trend in earnings since the late 1970s. But two new items, electronics and garments, became important export earners by 1980 and were the major source behind the growth in export earnings during the 1980-93 period. Over the same 1980-93 period, the share of coconut, sugar, forest and mineral products in total export earnings fell from 51 to 9 percent, while the share of electronics increased from 12 to 31 percent and that of garments, from 9 to 20 percent.

The imports consist mostly of consumer goods, machinery and transport equipment, mineral fuels, chemicals, food and live animals, and crude materials excluding fuels; in that order of importance. In the 1970s, the imports of mineral fuels accounted for more than one-fourth of the total import bill, which has shrunk to 12 percent by the early 1980s due to the stagnation of the industrial sector and the decline in oil prices in the world market. Once industrial activities pick up, mineral fuels will again become important component of the import bill. The Filipino people prefer imported durable products, irrespective of quality, to domestic manufactures and the large crowd in duty-free shops by returning overseas workers and their relatives is a common sight. The share of consumer goods in the total import bill has been increasing consistently since the mid-1970s.

Table 4.4
Growth and composition of external trade 1976-93

Variable	Year			
	1976	1980	1986	1993
Export earnings (percent of GNP)	15.1	17.9	16.6	20.5
Composition of exports (as percent of earnings)				
Coconut products	21.0	14.0	8.1	4.3
Sugar products	17.8	11.4	1.0	1.1
Forest products	12.0	8.1	3.7	0.4
Mineral products	11.9	17.8	5.4	3.2
Electronics	-	11.6	20.9	31.2
Garments	1.1	8.6	18.6	20.0
Import payments (percent of GNP)	23.3	25.6	18.4	33.8
Composition of imports (as percent of import bill)				
Machinery and transport equipment	29.3	23.6	15.6	32.7
Consumer goods	21.0	26.5	38.0	34.3
Mineral fuels	23.9	28.4	17.1	11.5
Chemicals	10.0	9.8	14.4	9.7
Food and live animals	8.7	6.9	8.5	6.8
Trade balance (percent of GNP)	8.2	7.7	1.8 1	5.3

Source: Asian Development Bank, 1994; *Key Indicators of Developing Asian and Pacific Countries*, Economic and Development Resource Center, Manila.

The deficit in the balance of payments amounted to nearly 8 percent of the GNP in the 1970s, which was financed with easy availability of foreign aids and loans till the end of the decade. But with increasing debt service liabilities and the tight foreign aid situation after the second oil price shock, it became difficult for the government to manage the balance of payment situation. The government resorted to devaluation of the peso to reduce the gap in the balance of trade. The exchange rate was depreciated from P8.54 per US dollar in 1982 to 20.4 by 1986, which had the desired effect of reducing the import bill from 25.6 percent of the GNP in 1980 to 18.4 percent by 1986. It did however, not have much effect on increasing export earnings as most of the exports were primary products with inelastic foreign demand and domestic supply. In fact, the export earnings also fell from 17.9 percent to 16.6 percent of the GNP. For imports, the impact was more on capital goods and raw materials than on consumer manufacturers thereby adversely affecting the industrial sector. The trade gap narrowed substantially to 1.8 percent of the GNP by 1986, but it could not be sustained. Imports again started growing at a much faster rate than exports, and by 1993, the negative trade balance reached 15.3 percent of the GNP. The growing trade gap is being financed with increasing flow of short-term, private foreign investment and remittances from workers employed overseas.

Unemployment and poverty

The combined forces of rapid growth in labor force and the slow pace of employment generation in productive sectors created a large pool of unemployed and underemployed workers. The unemployment rate remained low in the 1970s at 4-5 percent of the labor force, but increased to 7 percent by 1985 and to 9 percent during the 1991-93 period. The deceleration in the growth of productivity of the main cereals--rice and corn,--and the contraction of the export markets for agriculture-based products, coupled with the arduous nature of farm jobs pushed literate workers to move out from farm to nonfarm occupations and from rural to urban areas. This tended to depress real wages outside the farm, especially for unskilled occupations in the informal services sector. The decline in real wages was much faster for skilled and unskilled workers in the nonfarm sector than for agricultural laborers[8].

Increasing unemployment and declining wage rates imply deteriorating living conditions of the poor people. Table 4.5 shows the extent of poverty in the Philippines during the 1961-91 period. For the level of per capita incomes, the Philippines has a large proportion of poor people estimated at 65 percent for rural areas and 47 percent for urban areas. This is mainly because of the high concentration of assets and income. The Gini Coefficient of income distribution is estimated at 0.38 for rural areas and 0.43 for urban areas. Available evidence does not show any direct relationship between economic growth and incidence of poverty. During the 1960 when economic growth was impressive, the inequity in income distribution became more acute particularly in rural areas, but there was substantial improvement in the poverty situation. The higher income groups benefited more from the growth, but because rate of growth was impressive, some benefits also reached the poor. But it is interesting to note that during the economic recession in the 1980s, the improvement in poverty situation continued which may partly be due to the reduction in income inequality in rural areas as shown by the decline in the Gini Coefficient. It suggests that the middle and upper income group may have been hurt more by the economic recession than the lower income groups.

Table 4.5
Incidence of poverty in the Philippines 1961-88

Year	Percent of poor people		Gini concentration ratio	
	Rural	Urban	Rural	Urban
1961	80.2	65.0	0.39	0.51
1965	71.2	57.4	0.41	0.50
1971	66.1	51.3	0.45	0.44
1985	63.3	52.0	0.38	0.44
1988	54.1	40.0	0.38	0.43

Source: Balisacan (1992, 1994).

Macropolicies and economic management

Industrial policy

The Philippines followed an import substitution industrialization strategy that continued to dominate industrial policy until the early 1980s and greatly influenced the formulation of government policy in other sectors of the economy. A 1950 legislation required licensing for all imports and established controls on foreign exchange allocation by an Import Control Board. These measures created an industrial oligarchy who oriented their production toward the domestic market and established an inefficient industrial structure based on extraction of rents under the umbrella of import protection.

Baldwin[9] argued that industrial growth was significantly accelerated during the 1950s by the import substitution policies of the government. But once the relatively easy type of import substitution was over, the growth in the manufacturing sector as well as in the economy as a whole declined. There was considerable distortion in resource allocation created by these inward-looking policies and the bias toward capital-intensive production reduced the scope of employment generation. The bill on account of imports of capital equipment and raw materials exceeded the savings of foreign exchange from domestic production of potentially importable consumer goods and contributed to widening the gap in the balance of trade. In early 1960s, faced with foreign exchange shortage, allegation of corruption in import licensing and foreign exchange allocation, and pressure from landed interests and exporters of agro-based products, the government undertook a policy of phased elimination of the import control system and devalued the currency by almost 100 percent.

Since the mid-1960s, then a policy of export promotion in identified "pioneer" with new products or processes and preferred with substantial excess capacity industries was followed without changing the structure of trade protection. The Investment

Incentives Act of 1967 established the Board of Investment to determine investment priorities, process applications, and administer incentives. The Export Incentives Act of 1970 extended support to registered exporting firms in the form of tax exemptions, duty free imports of capital equipment, and duty drawbacks on imported intermediate goods. The export incentives were further extended in the 1970s by presidential decrees establishing export processing zones and bonded warehouses with a preferential rediscounting facility at the central bank on credit for export financing. The unrealistic exchange rate policy and the duty-free importation of capital goods created a capital-intensive bias in industrial development. The structure of exports shifted away from agro-based industries heavily dependent on the use of domestic raw materials to industries with very low value added component based on imported raw materials and capital goods. This partly explains the slow growth of industrial employment and value added in spite of a rapidly expanding foreign trade sector.

Although the need to promote an outward-looking, internationally competitive industrialization process has been recognized since the late 1960s, a serious effort at reforming the structure of trade protection was made only in the beginning of the 1980s. A program for gradual reduction of tariff rates, movement from quantitative restrictions on imports to control through tariffs, abolition of export taxes, and reforms of indirect tax system were part of the first World Bank structural adjustment loan contracted in 1981. The policy reforms were, however, implemented half-heartedly and in an incoherent manner. In a review of trade and industrial policy during the 1986-89 period, Medalla[10] concludes that minimal changes have been made in the tariff rates and the structure of trade protection has hardly changed. Another attempt at simplification of the tariff system and trade liberalization in 1990 met stiff opposition from vested interest groups who are politically powerful and have always exerted pressure on the administration to avert policies that hurt them.

Agricultural policy

Government interventions in the agricultural sector aimed at achieving several, often conflicting objectives, to stabilize foodgrain prices, raise farm incomes, maintain low prices of wage goods for urban consumers and industrial workers, and to attain self-sufficiency in foodgrains in the pursuit of food security. The level and nature of these government interventions and the relative importance of policy objectives have, however, changed over time in response to changes in the domestic demand and supply situations of the staple grain, the macroeconomic environment, and the political economy forces. The policy instruments consisted of price policies to influence the incentive structure, public expenditures for irrigation, research and extension to increase farm productivity, and land reforms to improve the distribution of incomes from rice and corn farming.

Domestic rice prices have been influenced by the government monopoly in an international trade and domestic marketing operations under the National Food

Authority (NFA). The NFA projects the demand-supply gap and sets the level of external trade to maintain a politically acceptable price level. Quantitative trade restrictions were also imposed on import of fertilizers in the early 1970s but were lifted in 1986. Import tariffs and advance sales tax were imposed on other tradeable inputs such as farm machinery and pesticides. The advance sales tax was abolished in 1986, but import tariffs continue to drive a wedge between domestic and border prices of tradeable inputs.

The impact of the price intervention policies was measured by Intal and Power[11] by estimating the trend in the nominal and effective protection rates. During the 1960s, the nominal protection rates were lower for inputs than for outputs, hence, effective protection was positive. During the 1970-84 period, the nominal protection for rice was negative while the domestic prices for inputs continued to be higher than the border prices, which resulted in negative price incentives for rice farmers. The continued downward trend in the price of rice in the world market with an upward trend in domestic prices has turned the nominal protection rate positive since 1985, but the negative effective protection rate continued till the end of the 1980s. The price incentives again turned in favor of the farmers during the 1990-94 period.

The government also invested heavily during the 1970s for the development of irrigation facilities. The government constructed, operated, and maintained large surface water-based irrigation systems. Although irrigation fees are charged to farmers, actual collections do not fully cover the cost of operation and maintenance, and the investment costs are fully subsidized. At its peak in 1979/80, the expenditure for irrigation accounted for 20 percent of total public expenditure for infrastructure development and 40 percent of the expenditure for the agricultural sector. With the sharp drop in world rice prices, severe budgetary squeeze and debt service problems since the early 1980s[12], public expenditure for the development and maintenance of irrigation facilities fell sharply in real terms, which was the main contributing factor to deceleration in the growth in rice yields since 1984.

The Marcos government enacted land reforms in 1972 by imposing ceilings on landholding at 7.0 has to improve the economic conditions of the tenants. The reforms stipulated that share tenants who worked from a landholding of more than 7.0 could purchase the land they tilled, while those on holdings of less than 7.0 would become leaseholders. Certificates of land transfer (CLTs) were issued to tenants and emancipation patents (EP) were to be granted to new owner when they complete compensation payment to the former landowner. The program, however, was applicable only to rice and corn farms where the concentration of land ownership was less acute. The plantation crops were left outside the purview of the land reforms. During the 1972-85 period, CLTs were issued on only 755,000 out of which only 12,000 were covered by EP.

The Aquino government (1986-92) instituted a Comprehensive Agrarian Reform Program (CARP) in 1987, which covered all agricultural lands, but had limited impact because of various exemptions, loopholes in legal provisions, and weak and slow implementation. Only 293,000 hectare of land were distributed to 173,000 farmer-beneficiaries. While both reform programs intended to reduce share tenancy, the proportion of tenant farmers and the incidence of tenancy actually increased during the 1971-91 period.

Monetary policy

The Philippines has one of the least developed financial systems in Southeast Asia. In 1987, the money supply was only 22 percent of the GNP in the Philippines, compared with 31 percent in Indonesia, 67 percent in Thailand, 75 percent in Malaysia and 85 percent in Singapore. The money market is characterized by the government's repression of asset prices, subsidized equity programs for private development banks, and an oligopolist commercial banking system nurtured by the Central Bank's aversion to the entry of foreign banks.

The policy regime in the financial market has gone through three phases. During the 1956-73 period, the government allowed market forces to operate in the money market while controlling the intermediation of surplus funds through the banking system. Lending rates were governed by the Usury Act of 1916 which prescribed ceilings on interest at 12 and 15 percent, respectively, for secured and unsecured loans. The deposit rates were fixed at low levels and hardly adjusted with changing inflation rates. During 1974-81, the coverage of the central bank's authority was broadened to include the pricing of assets and the structure of all financial institutions involved in credit allocation. While rates on long-term deposits were deregulated, the Central Bank continued to specify interest ceilings on short-term instruments. Incentives for intermediation in the money market were dampened by a reserve requirement of 20 percent of deposits of commercial banks and non-bank financial institutions and a 35 percent transaction tax on all primary borrowings in the money market. Beginning in 1981, a mix of free and administered market policies have been promoted with lifting of ceilings on interest rates, but further control of financial intermediation through the imposition of record high reserve requirements and taxes on deposit transactions. In 1984, the reserve requirement was raised to 24 percent, and a 5 percent tax on gross receipts of banks and a 20 percent tax on deposits and money market earnings of depositors/investors were imposed. These taxes comprised 25-39 percent of the average intermediation cost of the banks.

The trend in the nominal rates of deposit and lending rates of interest can be seen in Table 4.6. It also compares the interest rates with the rate of inflation in the country. The real rates of interests on savings deposits have almost always been negative. The lending rates were raised and kept at high levels throughout the 1980s. The difference in interest rates between time deposits and loan and advances were raised from less than 5 percent in the 1970s to around 10 percent during the 1980s. This large gap is due not only to the high rates of taxes on financial intermediation but also to the oligopolistic nature of the financial market. The system thus discouraged

Table 4.6
Trends in nominal and real rates of interest 1965-93
(percent per annum)

Variable	Year				
	1965-73	1974-80	1980-86	1987-91	1992-93
Deposit rates					
Savings deposit	5.9	7.6	9.5	4.6	9.5
Time deposit	6.7	10.7	12.9	13.8	11.5
Lending rate	12.0	12.9	20.0	19.3	17.0
Inflation rate	11.2	13.7	17.1	11.0	7.2
Real rate of interest	-4.5	-3.0	-4.2	-2.8	4.3
Gap between deposit and lending rates	5.3	2.2	7.1	5.5	5.5

Source: Asian Development Bank. 1994. *Key Indicators of Developing Asian and Pacific Countries.* Economic and Development Resource Center, Manila, Philippines. National Statistics Coordination Board, *Philippine Statistical Yearbook*, various issues.

mobilization of savings and financing of investments by small-scale entrepreneurs who have little access to financial institutions.

Fiscal policy

In the Philippines, fiscal policy is characterized by an expansion of the public sector, an inelastic and regressive tax system dependent on indirect taxes on domestic manufacturers and imported goods, and financing of growing fiscal deficits with loans initially from foreign and later from domestic capital markets.

The expansion of the public sector in the economy that took place throughout the 1970s was mainly to consolidate the political base of the ruling elite during the Marcos regime. In fact, much of the growth in public investments and the consolidated public deficits during the 1970-84 period could be traced to increased presence of public corporations. In the post-Marcos era, however, the increase in public expenditure was mainly due to the inflation of the debt service liabilities which increased from 1.8 percent of GNP in 1982 to about 10 percent by 1990.

The tax structure of the Philippines can be seen from Table 4.7. The tax revenue remained almost stagnant at around 12 percent of the GNP until 1988. During the Marcos regime, property taxes were almost insignificant and income taxes accounted

Table 4.7
Tax structure of the Philippines 1975-93

Source of government revenue	1975 % of GNP	1975 % share	1983 % of GNP	1983 % share	1988 % of GNP	1988 % share	1993 % of GNP	1993 % share
Taxes	12.0	81.8	11.0	87.3	11.4	80.0	15.3	8.8
Income	2.8	18.9	2.5	19.8	3.5	24.2	5.0	28.7
Property	0.0	0.2	0.1	0.7	0.0	0.3	0.0	0.9
Excise and sales	3.2	21.6	3.6	28.7	4.1	28.5	4.4	25.3
International trade	5.9	39.8	4.5	36.2	3.2	22.7	5.5	31.8
Other	0.2	1.3	0.2	1.9	0.5	3.3	0.4	2.5
Non-tax revenue	2.7	18.2	1.6	12.7	2.8	19.9	2.0	11.6
Total	1.47	100.0	12.6	100.0	14.2	100.0	17.3	100.0

Source: National Statistics Coordination Board, *Philippine Statistical Yearbook*, various issues.

for less than one-fifth of total tax revenue. The government heavily depended on its income on sales and excise taxes on domestic manufacturers, which accounted for nearly a fourth of the public revenue and on taxes on imports and exports contributing another two-fifths to the government exchequer. The income from public corporations declined from 19 percent of total revenue in 1975 to 13 percent in 1983 in spite of the rapid expansion of government control on economic activities. This indicates a trend of growing inefficiency in the operation of public enterprises. In the post-1986 period, however, there has been a commendable effort to increase public revenue through increasing efficiency in the collection of income and trade taxes, while at the same time reducing the rates of import tariffs and elimination of export taxes. The share of income taxes increased from 20 to 29 percent during the 1983-93 period, while the share of trade taxes decreased from 36 to 23 percent due to rationalization and reduction of tariff rates. The revenue from trade taxes increased to 32 percent by 1993 due to increased efficiency in the collection of these taxes.

Sustaining economic recovery

The present government which came to power in 1992 has already made significant improvement in economic management, consolidated political power, and strengthened democratic institutions that created a base for sustained economic recovery. The inflation rate has come down to 5.7 percent, exports increased by 16 percent in 1994 and 26 percent in the first quarter of 1995, while imports grew at 9 percent. There has been a dramatic increase in the inflow of private foreign investment. The power failure almost disappeared because of the personal attention given by the President to the energy sector. The GDP registered a growth of 4.1 percent in 1994 against a 2.1 percent increase in 1993 and is expected to rise to 5.4 percent in 1995. The growth was based on improved fiscal performance and liberalized trade and financial policies.

Several areas, however, need continued attention to sustain economic recovery. One potential weak area is the government's plan for infrastructure development which has been the key factor behind the economic recession. The public sector program for infrastructure development proposed in the Medium-Term Development Plan for 1993-98 is shown in Table 4.8. The growth in public expenditure for infrastructure development is planned at 7.7 percent per year which is totally inadequate to support a 7-9 percent targeted growth in national income by the terminal year of the plan. The allocation for energy and power sector is projected to grow at only 3 percent per year, while the expenditure for the communication sector is expected to decline by 25 percent. Only the transport and water resource sectors are expected to grow at 14 percent per year. Total public expenditure for infrastructure development is in fact projected to decline from 4.7 to 3.8 percent of the GNP. The relative reduction in public expenditure may be due to the government's policy of gradually shifting the responsibility of infrastructure development from the public to the private sector. The policy may, however, adversely affect the backward regions and low-income groups and stifle economic growth and accentuate income distribution. Since infrastructure is so underdeveloped and has long been neglected, it must be treated as a high priority area for government involvement.

Another area of weakness is the continuing reliance on foreign investment to finance the trade and current account deficits and to make up for the country's low saving rate which is still substantially below the level reached in the late 1970s. The government must give attention to reduce the import bill on account of consumer goods to eliminate the trade gap, and at the same time, increase the real rates of interest on deposits to encourage and mobilize domestic savings. The government is also going to rely heavily on the private sector for the planned increase in savings and investment rates from 17.6 percent of GNP in 1993 to 27.8 percent by 1998 as seen in Table 4.8. This target will be hard to realize unless there is further improvement in efficiency in the financial sector which should reduce the existing large gap between the lending and the deposit rate of interest and provide greater access with regard to credit to small-scale entrepreneurs. The government should also continue its efforts to mobilize more revenue from improving efficiency in tax collection and modernizing the indirect tax system, and to contain the growth in public services to increase its capacity to finance infrastructure development. The medium-term development plan in fact projects a decline in public savings from 6.3 percent of the GNP in 1993 to 5.8 percent by 1998.

Table 4.8
Projected growth in savings and investment 1993-98
(percent per annum)

Variable	Year and type		
	Average 1987-92	Actual 1993	Planned 1998
Foreign savings	2.7	5.9	1.7
Domestic savings			
Private	16.6	17.2	23.8
Public	4.4	6.3	5.8
Investments			
Private	16.3	13.9	21.1
Public	2.1	3.7	6.7

Source: Republic of the Philippines, 1993. *Medium-term Philippine Development Plan,* 1993-98.

Implementation of sound macroeconomic policies will need strengthening of democratic institutions, reducing dependence of politics on vested interest groups, removing bottlenecks in the legal and regulatory systems so that institutions are capable of designing and enforcing non-arbitrary sets of rules to guide economic activity, and improvement in the law and order situations through reducing political conflicts. There has been significant achievement in these areas over the last three years and much more remains to be done. Implementation of land reform to reduce the influence of landed interests and local power structure in the political system may contribute greatly to the development of the sociopolitical infrastructure needed for efficient macroeconomic management to sustain high rates of economic growth.

Notes

1   The author acknowledges the contribution of Thelma Paris and Josephine Narciso in compilation of available documents and analysis of data. International Rice Research Institute is not responsible for opinions expressed in this paper.

2   For details, see reports of *The Philippine Census of Agriculture.*

3   National Statistics Coordination Board, *Philippine Statistical Yearbook,* various issues.

4   A.M. Balisacan, et al, *Perspective on Philippine Poverty*, 1993, Center for Integrative and Development Studies, UP Diliman and Council on Southeast Asian Studies, Yale University.

5   S.A. Resnick, "The Decline of Rural Industry Under Export Expansion: A Comparison Among Burma, Philippines, and Thailand, 1970-83, *Journal of Economic History*, vol.30, no. 1, pp. 51-73.

6   M. Kikuchi, *Export Oriented Garment Industries in Rural Philippines*, 1994, Chiba University, Tokyo.

7   Ibid.

8   A.M. Balisacan, "Economic Modernization, Market Responses, and Rural Welfare in the Philippines", paper presented at the conference on *Social Science Methods in Agricultural Systems Research: Coping with Increasing Resource Competition in Asia*, 1994, Chiang Mai, Thailand.

9   R. Baldwin, *Foreign Trade Relations and Economic Development: The Philippines*, 1975, National Bureau of Economic Research, New York.

10 E.M. Medalla, "An Assessment of Trade and Industrial Policy 1986-88 ", PIDS, *Working Paper Series* no. 90-07, 1990.

11 P.S. Intal and J. Power, " The Philippines" in A.O. Krueger, et al eds. *The Political Economy of Agricultural Pricing Policy*, 1991, Johns Hopkins University Press, Baltimore and London.

12 See later.

References

Asian Development Bank.   1992.   Study on Foodcrop Policies, Manila,The Philippines. Philippines.

Asian Development Bank.   1994.   Key Indicators of Developing Asian and Pacific Countries. Economic and Development Resource Center, Manila, The Philippines.

Baldwin, R., *Foreign Trade Regions and Economic Development: The Philippines*, 1975, National Bureau of Economic Research, New York.

Balisacan A. M., Economic Modernization, Market Responses, and Rural Welfare in the Philippines. Paper presented at the conference on *Social Science Methods in Agricultural Systems Coping with Increasing Resource Competition in Asia*, 1994, Chiang Mai, Thailand, November 2-4, 1994.

Balisacan, A.M., et al, *Perspective of Philippine Poverty*, 1993, Center for Integrative and Development Studies, UP Diliman and Council on Southeast Asian Studies, Yale University.

85

Balisacan, A. M., Rural Poverty in the Philippines: Incidence, Determinants and Policies, pp 125-163 in *Asian Development Review, Studies of Asian and Pacific Economic Issues,* 1992, vol. 10 no.1. Asian Development Bank.

Intal, P.S. and Power, J., "The Philippines", in A.O. Krueger, et al eds., *The Political Economy of Agricultural Pricing Policy,* 1991, Johns Hopkins University Press, Baltimore, London.

Kikuchi, M., *Export-oriented Garment Industries in Rural Philippines,* 1994. Chiba University, Tokyo, Japan.

Medalla, E. M., "An Assessment of Trade and Industrial Policy, 1986-1988," *PIDS Working Paper Series,* no. 90-07, January, 1990.

National Statistical Coordination Board (NSCB, various issues. 1994, Philippine Statistical Yearbook, Manila.

National Statistical Coordination Board (NSCB), various issues. 1994, *Philippine Statistical Yearbook,* Manila.

Power, T., and G. Sicat, *The Philippines: Industrialization and Trade Policies,* 1971, New York, London, OECD Development Center.

Republic of the Philippines, *Medium-Term Philippine Development Plan* 1993-98, 1993, Manila, Philippines

Resnick, S.A., *The decline of rural industry under export expansion: a comparison among Burma, Philippines and Thailand,* 1870-1938, 1970, vol. 30, no.1, pp. 51-73.

5 A brief assessment of Singapore's economic miracle

Habibullah Khan
National University of Singapore

Abstract

After reviewing Singapore's economic performance in the past three decades, this chapter seeks to identify the reasons for Singapore's success, by adopting a political economy approach. It is argued that Singapore adopted a 'balanced' combination of market and government and its economic philosophy closely reflected the "governed market" theory based on "developmental state" model. Although government intervention in Singapore was fairly extensive, the interventionist measures did not distort market efficiency due to high quality of political leadership, pragmatism, meritocracy and social conformism. The future outlook for Singapore economy remains bright and such an optimism is based on improvements in its educational standards, training programs, and stringent criteria of recruitment in the administrative service, as argued in the chapter.

Introduction

Rapid growth in Singapore for the past three decades is viewed by most[1] as an 'economic miracle.' The size of the economy in 1993, as measured by real GDP, was nearly eleven times[2] that in 1965--the year when Singapore attained political independence. On an average, the economy grew 8.8 percent annually during this period and consistently maintained an upward trend with only two exceptions. In 1975, the economy experienced a slow real growth of only 4 percent due mainly to oil price shock. Again in 1985, the economy underwent a short recessionary period and the growth rate fell to minus 1.6 percent for the first time in the history of Singapore. A number of corrective measures, based on the recommendations of a high-powered economic committee[3], were undertaken immediately and the economy returned to its normal growth path in less than two years.

Singapore not only enjoyed high economic growth but growth here has been accompanied by full employment, high savings and investment rates, nearly 85 percent home-ownership ratio, a healthy balance of payments and growing foreign exchange reserves, a strong currency, and a low inflation rate. There is little doubt that Singapore has set an example of how a small city state can be transformed into an economically powerful nation within a short span of time. In the World Bank classification, Singapore is listed in the "higher-income economies" group with a per capita gross national product (GNP) even higher than some developed nations, such as Ireland, New Zealand and Spain.[4]

What caused Singapore's success? This question was asked by many who sought to explain the East Asian economic miracle, particularly the phenomenal growth in "Four Asian Dragons" such as Singapore, Hong Kong, South Korea, and Taiwan, and the search for an appropriate answer led to the emergence of two important paradigms in development economics.[5] The dominant paradigm usually called "Neoclassical political economy" is based on a market-oriented explanation and it maintains that the East Asian success provides a clear demonstration of vigorous market competition and free trade as the twin 'engines of growth'. The alternative view often labeled "New political economy" stresses the role of government in East Asia and thus provides the notion of the state as an engine of growth. The paper examines Singapore's economic performance in the light of these two competing paradigms and argues that a 'balanced' combination of market and government is required for success. Although government intervention in Singapore was fairly extensive, the interventionist measures did not distort market efficiency due to high quality of political leadership, pragmatism, meritocracy, and social conformism, as argued in the paper.

Economic performance of Singapore 1965-93

The highly-acclaimed success of Singapore in achieving rapid economic growth is displayed in Table 5.1. The first five years following independence in 1965, the city-state experienced a record growth rate of nearly 12 percent per annum. Quite surprisingly, the high growth of real GDP sustained for the entire period of Singapore's history, although the rate of expansion gradually diminished over the years until about 1992. The growth rate again entered into a double-digit phase in 1993 when the economy registered just about 10 percent real GDP growth. Although the data for 1994 is yet to be finalized, the growth rate in the year is expected to exceed 10 percentage points. The future outlook based on medium-term projections, also seems quite robust.

Although the periodic growth figures consistently show an upward trend, the yearly data indicates that Singapore also has had two 'bad years'. In 1975, Singapore's real GDP growth plummeted to a meager 4 percent. It was precipitated by the oil price shock which triggered off a worldwide recession. External demand fell and as

Table 5.1

Per annum growth rates of main economic indicators for Singapore

Indicator	Year					
	1965-70	1971-80	1981-90	1990-91	1991-92	1992-93
Real GDP[1]	11.9	9.1	7.1	6.7	6.0	9.9
Inflation rate[2]	1.5	6.3	2.8	3.5	2.1	2.4
Savings ratio[3]	17.2	29.0	41.5	47.4	48.2	47.5
Investment ratio[3]	26.4	41.2	42.2	38.0	40.4	43.8

Notes: 1)Based on GDP at 1985 market prices; 2)Annual percentage change in GDP deflators (1985=100); 3)The savings ratio and investment ratio are defined respectively as gross national savings and gross capital formation divided by gross domestic product at current market prices. Sources: *Singapore National Accounts,* 1987, Department of Statistics, Singapore, 1988; *Singapore Yearbook of Statistics,* 1993, Department of Statistics, Singapore, 1994.

incomes dropped, domestic activities were also adversely affected. Another bad year for Singapore was 1985 when the economy experienced a real GDP contraction of 1.6 percent. Since the country was not accustomed to such bad times and as high growth was virtually taken for granted, the 1985 recession shocked everybody. A high-powered economic committee was appointed by the government immediately to investigate the reasons for such a severe recession and it was found by the committee that the erosion of Singapore's cost-competitiveness vis-à-vis its trading partners coupled with other adverse domestic factors such as over-supply in the hyperactive construction sector mainly caused the downturn. The various cost-cutting measures introduced by the government in the mid-1985 together with the policy of wage restraint helped restore Singapore's international competitiveness, and the economy returned to its normal growth path by the end of 1987.[6]

The sustained economic growth and gradual appreciation of Singapore dollar have resulted in Singapore having the highest per capita GNP among developing countries. By the later part of the 1970s, Singapore had been variously labeled as a middle-income country, an advanced developing country, a semi-industrialized country, and a newly industrialized economy (NIE). There was growing concern amongst the political leaders over the premature graduation of Singapore as a 'developed' country and the consequent loss of 'Generalized System of Preferences (GSP)' benefits. It was argued that because of the large foreign presence in Singapore, a per capita GNP based on the indigenous Singaporean component better reflects the level of development and standard of living in the city-state republic.[7] It may also be argued that the per capita income of a small city-state is likely to be higher than a regionally diverse country with large rural sector because of the higher degree of monetisation and higher costs of living in a city.

Due to the well-known limitations of per capita GNP as a general measure of economic development, the international agencies have been using various economic and social indicators for measuring levels of living for quite sometime. Table 5.2 presents a set of such indicators for Singapore and a few other selected countries. It can be clearly observed that Singapore is far more developed than its ASEAN counterparts. The striking similarity between Singapore and Hongkong is also clearly visible from the data. Although Singapore is still far below other highly advanced nations such as Switzerland and Japan in terms of per capita GNP, it seems to be quickly 'catching up' in terms of other measures such as life expectancy, infant mortality, access to medical facilities, access to safe water, and so on. One gets an

Table 5.2

Selected development indicators for Singapore and a few other countries
(latest available years; values expressed in US$)

Country	GNP	Grow	Infln	Lifex	Illit	Infant	Doctor	Low20	Phone	Water
Australia	17260	1.6	6.4	77	<5[a]	7	830[b]	4.4	456	100
Canada	20710	1.8	4.1	78	<5[a]	7	450	5.7	577	100
Greece	7290	1.0	17.7	77	7	8	580	n.a.	391	98
Hongkong	15360	5.5	7.8	78	n.a.	6	1510[b]	5.4	434	100
Indonesia	670	4.0	8.4	60	23	66	7030	8.7	6	51
Italy	20460	2.2	9.1	77	<5[a]	8	210	6.8	388	100
Japan	28190	3.6	1.5	79	<5[a]	5	610	8.7	441	96
S. Korea	6790	8.5	5.9	71	4	13	1070	7.4	310	93
Malaysia	2790	3.2	2.0	71	22	14	2590	4.6	89	78
New Zealand	12300	0.6	9.4	7	<5[a]	7	870[b]	5.1	437	97
Philippines	770	-1.0	14.1	65	10	40	8120	6.5	10	81
Portugal	7450	3.1	17.4	74	15	9	490	n.a.	241	92
Singapore	15730	5.3	2.0	75	10	5	820	5.1	385	100
Spain	13970	2.9	8.7	77	5	8	280	8.3	323	100
Switzerland	36080	1.4	3.8	78	<5[a]	6	630	5.2	587	100
Thailand	1840	6.0	4.2	69	7	26	4360	6.1	24	77
U.K.	17790	2.4	5.7	76	<5[a]	7	810	4.6	442	100
U.S.A.	23240	1.7	3.9	77	<5[a]	9	420	4.7	545	n.a

Notes: GNP-Per capita GNP, 1992; GROW-Average annual growth rate, 1980-92; INFLN-Average annual rate of inflation, 1980-92; LIFEX-Life expectation at birth (years), 1992; ILLIT-Adult illiteracy (male plus female), 1990; INFANT-Infant mortality rate (per 1000 live births), 1992; DOCTOR-Population per physician, 1990; LOW20- Percentage share of income by lowest 20 percent, latest available year; PHONE-Telephones per 1000 population, 1990; WATER-Percentage of population with access to safe water, 1990; a-according to UNESCO, illiteracy is less than 5 percent; b-data for 1970.
Main Source: The World Bank, *World Development Report,* 1994, Oxford University Press, London 1994.

impression from Table 5.2 that Singapore has already become a 'developed' country, although there is some reluctance on the part of political leaders to admit this fact due mainly to the anticipated loss of trade concessions.

Besides rising standards of living, several other features can be discerned from Singapore's growth experience. First of all, economic growth was accompanied by fundamental structural transformation. Two important changes that occurred in the past three decades can be noticed from the data presented in Table 5.3. The share of manufacturing in total output increased rapidly from 19.6 in 1965 to 29.5 percent in 1980 and remained more or less stable thereafter, with the exception of year 1985, when the share of manufacturing fell rather considerably due to economic recession.

Table 5.3
Percentage share of Singapore's GDP (1985 market prices)
by industrial sector 1965-90

Sector	Year							
	1965	1975	1980	1985	1990	1991	1992	1993
Agriculture & fishing	2.9	1.5	1.1	0.8	0.3	0.3	0.3	0.2
Quarrying	0.2	0.3	0.2	0.3	0.1	0.1	0.1	0.1
Manufacturing	19.6	26.0	29.5	23.6	28.9	28.5	27.6	27.6
Utilities	1.7	1.9	2.0	2.0	2.1	2.1	2.1	2.0
Construction	9.6	8.9	7.1	10.7	5.3	6.0	6.8	6.7
Commerce	21.6	20.9	18.9	17.0	18.0	18.4	18.2	17.9
Transport & communications	7.3	9.1	11.9	13.4	14.2	14.3	14.7	14.6
Financial & business services	16.5	20.0	20.3	27.1	26.1	26.3	26.1	26.9
Other services	19.5	13.8	11.8	12.0	10.3	10.3	10.2	9.8
Minus imputed bank service charge	1.1	3.0	4.7	8.2	6.2	7.4	7.0	6.8
Plus import duties	4.8	1.7	1.7	1.2	0.9	0.9	1.0	0.9
Total*	100	100	100	100	100	100	100	100
GDP at 1985 market prices	6626.8	19171.4	28832.5	38923.5	57271.9	61081	647710	712119

Note: *Figures may not add up to total due to rounding errors.
Sources: Department of Statistics, *Singapore National Accounts*, 1987; *Singapore Yearbook of Statistics*, 1993, Singapore.

The other structural change can be seen in the composition of the tertiary sector. Between 1965 and 1993 the first two components of the tertiary or services sector, namely, transport and communications, and financial and business services, grew quite consistently in terms of their GDP shares. The share of the third service component which includes public administration, community, social and personal services, however declined gradually in the same period and in 1993 it contributed less than 10 percent to Singapore's GDP. The share of the commerce sector also declined over the years but despite the fall in relative terms it still remains as one of the four Singapore's 'growth pillars'. The three other pillars of growth are manufacturing, financial and business services, and transportation and communications.

Secondly, the structure of trade--particularly, exports has changed drastically and Singapore has been transformed from a predominantly entrepot economy into an industrialized city-state economy. Due to its strategic location and good natural harbor, Singapore has long been serving as a vital trading post for countries in the Southeast Asian region, and in 1965 re-exports of the republic accounted for nearly 75 percent of the total exports (Table 5.4). The outward-looking industrialization drive undertaken in early 1970s shifted the emphasis away from the re-exports character to the direct export of Singapore-made manufactures, and in 1975 the share of re-exports to total exports fell to only 41 percent. Although re-exports still remain an important component of Singapore's international trade, domestic exports have grown quite sharply over the years and presently they account for nearly two-thirds of the republic's total exports. The success of the industrialization policy can perhaps be more clearly indicated by the rising share of manufactured exports as a percentage of total exports and in 1993 the share of manufacturing stood at nearly 80 percent. The data contained in Table 5.4 also suggest that Singapore has always been an extremely 'open' economy and its heavy reliance on international trade can be seen from export/ GDP and import/ GDP ratios. Thirdly, Singapore has experienced a balance of payments surplus virtually every year[8] since its independence. Although it has a persistent deficit in merchandise trade balance, the deficit has been more than outweighed by the huge surpluses in trade in services which include tourism, transportation, ship repairing and port services and by massive inflows of foreign capital. The obvious consequence of a positive balance of payments is the accumulation of foreign reserves and a strong Singapore dollar. The international reserves grew continuously from a meager US$430 million in 1965 to a staggering US$48.2 billion in 1993. In fact, Singapore's present level of foreign reserves is one of the highest in the world, as revealed by the data presented in Table 5.5.

Fourthly, Singapore's economic growth has been characterized by high savings as well as high investments. The savings rate, as measured by the ratio of gross national savings (GNS) to GDP, rose from 17.2 percent in 1965-70 to 47.5 percent in 1992-93 (Table 5.1). Both private and public sectors contributed to the high savings rate. Private savings have largely been boosted by the compulsory contributions[9] to the Central Provident Fund (CPF). The public sector[10] in Singapore is also a major saver

Table 5.4
Singapore's trade statistics 1965-93

Variable				Year				
Value in S$ million	1965	1975	1980	1985	1990	1991	1992	1993
Total exports	3004	12758	41452	59179	95206	101880	103351	119473
Re-exports	2239	5218	15647	19603	32452	35848	37014	44079
Domestic exports	765	7540	25805	32576	62754	66031	66337	75394
Manufactured exports(SITC 5-8)	935	5337	18522	26260	68854	74926	80379	94828
Total imports	3807	19270	51354	57818	109806	114195	117530	137603
GDP at current market price	2956	13373	24201	38448	66175	73038	79083	89007
Proportion in percent								
Re-exports/total exports	74.5	40.9	37.7	35.1	34.1	35.2	35.8	36.9
Domestic exports/ total exports	25.5	59.1	62.3	64.9	65.9	64.8	64.2	63.1
Total exports/GDP	101.6	95.4	171.3	130.5	143.9	139.5	130.7	134.2
Total imports/GDP	128.8	144.1	212.2	150.4	165.9	156.4	148.6	154.6
Manufactured exports/GDP	31.1	41.8	44.7	52.3	72.3	73.5	77.8	79.4

Source: Department of Statistics, *Singapore Yearbook of Statistics,* Singapore, various issues.

and its savings constitute government budgetary surpluses and the operating surpluses of various statutory boards. The investment rate, as measured by the ratio of gross fixed capital formation (GFCF) to GDP, also increased quite significantly from 26.4 percent in 1965-70 to 43.8 percent in 1992-93 (see Table 5.5). A large proportion of the investment went to the construction of infrastructure and buildings (for housing, industry and business). While the public sector played a major role in infrastructural and housing development, investments in commercial buildings, machinery and equipments were largely undertaken by the private sector.

Finally, Singapore's economic development occurred with remarkably low rates of inflation (Tables 1 and 2). The annual inflation rate averaged below 3 percent in every decade except the 1970s. Singapore's success in containing inflationary pressure arising from rising world prices led to the significant betterment of people's quality of life (by raising their real incomes) over the years.

Table 5.5
International reserves for Singapore and a few other countries
1965-93 (US$ million)

Year	Singapore	Japan	S. Korea	Taiwan	Switzerland
1965	430	1824	143	245	402
1970	1012	4308	606	480	2401
1975	3007	11950	781	1074	7019
1980	6567	24636	2925	2205	15659
1985	12847	26719	2869	22556	18016
1990	27748	78501	14793	72441	29223
1991	34133	72059	13701	82405	29004
1992	39885	71623	17121	82306	33255
1993	48191	98524	20228	n.a.	32635

Main Sources: International Monetary Fund, *International Financial Statistics Yearbook*, 1993; Republic of China, *Statistical Yearbook of the Republic of China*, 1993.

Explaining the success: market versus government

Two major schools of thought grew out of research undertaken in recent years to explain the East Asian economic miracles. The "market-supremacy" school, which is primarily based on the Neoclassical theory of markets and prices, has again produced two fairly distinct views on the roles of market and government in generating extraordinary growth, as experienced in the East Asian NIEs including Singapore. One view, which largely occupied the mainstream of the economics profession in the 1970s, suggests that the superior economic performance of the region can be attributed to their reliance on free markets. This "Free Market (FM)" theory of East Asian success claims that in countries such as Japan, Taiwan, Singapore and Hong Kong, growth is the result of more efficient allocation of resources which comes from more freely functioning markets.[11] State intervention in these countries is largely absent and what state provides is simply a suitable environment for the entrepreneurs to perform their functions more freely, as argued by the proponents of the theory.

Another view, which can be considered a variant of the core Neoclassical theory and is often known as the "Simulated free market (SFM)" theory of East Asian success, believes that the governments of East Asia intervened fairly widely to offset various distortions but the results of activist policies were very close to those that would have prevailed under free market situation in any way. The main reason for the success of the NIEs, according to this theory, is the adoption of a 'neutral' trade regime (as opposed to 'free' trade regime advocated by the FM theory), which ensures that the effects of import control measures would be counterbalanced by export promotion measures.[12]

These two market-oriented interpretations of East Asian economic performance have recently been challenged by a 'statist counter-revolution'. The central thesis of this new school of thought, often classified as "New political economy", is that the phenomenon of 'late development' should be understood as a process in which states have played a strategic role in taming domestic and international market forces and harnessing them to national ends. In other words, the key to rapid economic growth in East Asia is a strong and autonomous state, providing directional thrust to the operation of the market system. The market is guided by long-term national interests and key investment decisions are made by government officials. It is the "synergy" between the state and the market which provides the basis for rapid economic growth.

The statist model of East Asian political economy emerged from the concept of "developmental state"[13] which embodies the following characteristics: First, economic growth constitutes the foremost and single-minded priority of state action. Conflict of goals is avoided by the absence of any commitment to equality and social welfare. Second, there is an underlying commitment to private property and market, and state intervention is firmly circumscribed by this commitment. The market however is guided by an elite bureaucracy staffed by the best available managerial talent in the system. Within the bureaucracy, a pilot agency plays a key role in policy formulation and implementation. Third, Close institutionalized links are established between the elite bureaucracy and private business for consultation and cooperation. Fourth, An authoritarian political system in which the bureaucracy is given sufficient scope to take initiatives and operate effectively. The politicians "reign" while the bureaucrats "rule". Fifth, a cordial industrial relations system is established by implementing tough laws against union militancy and by adopting a sophisticated labor management style which encourages workers' loyalty to their bosses and competition among the workers themselves.

Based on the broad framework provided by Johnson's developmental state model, Wade[14] proposed a new theory, which he calls the "governed market (GM)" theory of East Asian success, as an alternative to the Neoclassical free market or simulated free market explanations. Unlike other theories, the GM theory is formulated in such a way that it can be tested with real-world data. It says that the superiority of East Asian economic performance is due in large measure to a combination of: (1) very high levels of productive investment, making for fast transfer of newer techniques into actual production; (2) more investment in certain key industries than would have occurred in the absence of government intervention; and (3) exposure of many industries to international competition, in foreign markets if not at home. These are the proximate causes. At a more fundamental level, these outcomes themselves are the causes of a specific set of policies which enable the government to "guide" or "govern" the process of resource allocation so as to produce a different production and investment profile than would result under a free market system. The set of incentives, controls, and mechanisms to spread risk, which may all be implemented under the banner of strategic industrial policy, are in turn supported by a certain kind of organizations of the state and the private sector. Wade claims that the corporatist[15] and authoritarian political arrangements of East Asia have provided the basis for market guidance.

Which model of East Asian economic success fits Singapore the most? Perhaps, the governed market theory based on the developmental state model, with little or no modifications at all, would closely reflect Singapore's economic philosophy. Being strongly efficiency-conscious and achievement-oriented, the government of Singapore right from the beginning regulated the private sector activities with various policy instruments in order to attain its long-term development objectives. Such an interventionist policy was clearly indicated by the then Deputy Prime Minister of Singapore, Dr. Goh Keng Swee,[16] in the following statement:

> ... the *laissez-faire* policies of the colonial era had led Singapore to a dead end, with little economic growth, massive unemployment, wretched housing and inadequate education. We had to try a more activist and interventionist approach. The roles of the government are not only to perform the traditional roles of a government-- defense, law and order, and to provide infrastructure for private enterprises--but also to participate actively in economic activities as well as to lay down clear guidelines to private sector as to what they could and should do.

The Singapore government had no ideological commitment to any particular economic system--free enterprise, socialism or whatsoever. Its only concern was the betterment of living for Singaporeans and in order to achieve this objective, it implemented a host of 'pragmatic' policies which involved extensive government intervention in several areas such as population control, housing, education, medical and health services, compulsory savings, industrial relations, wage policy, and so on. The economic pragmatism also motivated the government to adopt an open-door policy not only to foreign investment and technology, but also to foreign managers, engineers and technicians. Singapore never suffered from xenophobic post-colonial hangover. Moreover, there was a realization that, given its small size, it could not possibly develop a critical pool of high-level manpower required to run the economy. In the mid-1980s, it was estimated that foreign managers, engineers, and technicians constituted 20 percent of the workforce in these categories.[17] The same pragmatism also prompted the government to reject any prestigious project which has little returns e.g. steel mills and in souring foreign investment, to prefer MNCs from U.S.A., Japan, and Western Europe over MNCs from Hong Kong and Taiwan.[18]

The political leaders in Singapore firmly believe in the principle of meritocracy which dictates the systems of reward and advancement at various sociopolitical levels. The perception is that the country's progress depends quite heavily on its ability to identify the talents and groom them so as to develop their potentials to the fullest extent.[19] The belief in meritocracy has created a system by which only the 'best' in terms of educational qualifications and training can move up the ranks into the positions of power and responsibility and this in turn, according to many, has given rise to "elitism". Another by-product of meritocracy is the "government-knows-best" attitude, which is often reflected in the statements made by government officials and political leaders. Such an attitude may have also come about because the government has access to data and information[20] which are vital inputs to decision-making and evaluation of policies best suited for Singapore. The meritocratic style has also given rise to "paternalism" which characterizes the political leaders in Singapore. The paternalistic approach has led to government intervention in all areas including marriage, procreation, education, and so on.

It is clear from the above that the government of Singapore played a strong role in the economic development of the city-state republic. Although the share of government in GDP is not particularly large,[21] the qualitative impact of government's predominance can be felt everywhere. The government in Singapore has in fact played the roles of goal-setter, producer, regulator, and fiscal agent, in addition to its traditional roles as the custodian of the nation. While the rules of market mechanism remains paramount in Singapore, the government has interfered in a big way so as to ensure that the fruits of economic growth are more equally distributed. There is a progressive income tax where by most taxes are paid by the upper and middle-income groups. The subsidized public housing, education, health and medical services benefit mostly the lower-income groups.

However, the government does not believe in giving unemployment allowances or any other transfer payments as these transfer will undermine work incentives. Regarding the role of market, the prevailing perception in Singapore is that it can be used more effectively as an instrument of policies and goals rather than 'invisible hand' mechanism. For example, the government decides on the number of certificates of entitlement (COEs) for car ownership to be issued in each month but then uses auction mechanism to allocate them. Similarly, the government also decides on the amount of levies, overall number, and the source of foreign labor, but then allows this labor to be allocated to those who are prepared to pay the resulting price. Thus market is used as an instrument because it is regarded as more economical in information and administrative costs, but not as a mechanism. It should however be noted that such use of market does not carry with it the normative efficiency implications which are usually associated with market mechanism leading to so-called Pareto efficiency.[22] The policy makers in Singapore however did ensure that state intervention did not ignore the disciplining functions of the market. Moreover, state intervention led to the reduction of uncertainty and risks of business through overall policy stability.

Why state intervention was so successful?

With the exception of few East Asian NIEs such as Singapore, state interventionism failed to achieve good results, though it was applied extensively in most other developing countries. What made intervention work so well in Singapore? It is argued in this chapter that it is not state intervention *per se* that distinguishes Singapore as well as other East Asian NIEs from other less developed countries but it is the effectiveness of state intervention and quality of interventionist measures that made the crucial difference in results.

Effective state intervention to bring about economic as well as social transformation requires that the state is able to formulate and implement coherent economic and social policies. Formulation of such policies in turn will depend on the 'autonomy of the state' from the dominant class or various interest groups so that the state can pursue goals that do not reflect the interests of these groups and if necessary may even go against their short-term interests. Effective intervention also requires 'stability' which can be attained through efficient structuring of the state apparatus and by ensuring increasing material gains for the bulk of the population. The 'administrative capability' of the government leaders is also a crucial factor in determining the effectiveness of state intervention.

The first of the above three factors, the autonomy of government from interest groups, which was emphasized earlier by the proponents of developmental state hypothesis, can rarely be found in less developed countries (LDCs). The government of Singapore also initially faced the risks of being captured by certain interest groups backed by local Chinese business class who tried to promote China-oriented economic and social policies. The People's Action Party (PAP)[23] government led by Lee Kuan Yew successfully neutralized these interest groups, who even gained strong support of the leftist wing of the PAP, with the help of a carefully-designed combination of control mechanisms and achievement-oriented policies.

The English-educated Chinese leadership, headed by Lee, saw the future of Singapore in rapid economic growth achieved by the adoption of western technology and capital brought by MNCs from the west, not in inward-looking business and investment strategies advocated by the leaders of the Chinese business community. The Lee Kuan Yew government maintained the position that the adoption of a Hong Kong development model reliant on small Chinese manufacturing enterprise and some local entrepreneurs would be disastrous for Singapore as it would tend to perpetuate the serious unemployment problem which existed during the period of independence and the city-state would permanently be stuck with traditional entrepot trade activities yielding at best a modest economic growth. The idea received popular support and thus consolidated the position of the PAP government.

As far as stability is concerned, a stable political environment prevailed at the time of Singapore's independence, as the PAP government fully neutralized the opposition parties during the transition period, 1959-1965. When Singapore emerged as an independent nation on August 9, 1965, a stable government, competent administration, efficient institutions, and other factors needed for growth, were all in place. After independence, government extended and consolidated its control over the trade unions and the mass media. The Industrial Relations Act of 1968 played an important part in reducing the role of collective bargaining in Singapore, for it gave full discretionary powers to management in matters of promotion, transfer, recruitment, dismissal, reinstatement, assignment of duties and termination of employment for reasons of reorganization or redundancy. Further legislation in the Eighties gave employers greater flexibility in the use of labor force.[24] The National Wages Council (NWC), set up in 1979, also contributed significantly to ensure stability in the labor market by producing a more orderly and systematic wage behavior. To promote the overall stability, the government also imposed various restrictions on the mass media so that the credibility of the government could not be undermined by making unnecessary criticisms. The issue of press freedom was debated recently in Singapore and the government maintains the following position: "Singapore is not America. It is small and fragile and needs a strong and fair government to survive. If its government is continually criticized, vilified and ridiculed in the media, and pressured by lobbyists as in America, then the government will lose control. The result will not be more freedom, but confusion, conflict, and decline".[25]

Last but not the least, the administrative capability of Singapore's leaders was undoubtedly quite high. They have consistently been making good economic judgements and sound economic policies which resulted in unprecedented economic growth. A small group of leaders led by Lee Kuan Yew[26] dominated Singapore's politics right from the beginning and the distinguishing features of these men were their personal integrity, honesty, dedication, and a high level of formal education. Corruption, endemic in most less developed countries (LDCs), was virtually absent in Singapore.

The quality of interventionist policies applied to a particular sector or to the economy as a whole would depend on four key factors - 'flexibility', 'selectivity', 'coherence' and 'market friendliness'. Singapore's policies, economic or social, were characterized by these factors. Flexibility, for example, can be seen in the republic's changing industrial strategies. The first strategy, often called " labor-intensive import-substitution strategy", began in 1961 when protective measures such as tariffs and quotas were introduced, and this strategy continued until about 1968. The second strategy called "export-oriented manufacturing strategy" began in 1968-69 when Singapore moved largely toward free trade. Import restrictions imposed earlier were withdrawn and exchange controls eliminated. A new strategy, popularly known as "industrial restructuring" began in 1979 with policies for economic and technological upgrading. Flexibility[27] in industrial policies is also reflected in gradual shifts in 'priorities' announced by the Economic Development Board (EBB).

Like other successful East Asian countries, Singapore has adopted policies which have been highly selective, favoring certain industries or sectors in line with broad macroeconomic objectives. Projects are selected after careful evaluation, implemented with extreme precaution, and performance of the selected projects are then continuously reviewed.[28] Another feature of government policies is the high degree of coherence amongst them. There has always been broad agreement on economic goals,[29] and policies have been coordinated to achieve these goals. Finally, the government policies in Singapore have been directed toward the promotion rather than the regulation of private enterprises, and have been 'market-friendly' rather than 'market-repressing'. Even the public enterprises[30] are run on a commercial basis. They are expected to be efficient, make profits and expand whenever feasible. Government does not provide them with special privileges or subsidies. If they lose money, they are allowed to go bankrupt. It is the stated policy of the government not to buy failing firms--public or private just to save jobs.

Conclusion

Knowing that the government of Singapore intervened extensively in various economic and social areas, the question which naturally arises is: has government intervention been 'excessive'? Economic theory does not provide an answer to the question. This is not because economic theory is an imperfect corpus of knowledge but simply because there is no 'right' answer to the question. Factors which might influence the size of the government include socioeconomic conditions, ideological preferences, economic and political objectives, the capabilities of the government leaders, and the quality of private entrepreneurship. All these factors, excepting the last one, were considered in our earlier discussion on the pervasiveness of government role in Singapore. We now wish to comment briefly on the quality of private entrepreneurship.

There is a common contention that Singapore is seriously deficient in entrepreneurial activity. Local firms generally seem to be afflicted by low productivity and relatively inefficient management. Such a perception however needs to be carefully interpreted. Singapore has historically been a highly successful trade-based re-export economy and it is in such entrepot activities that local entrepreneurs have always thrived. The same can not be said about the manufacturing sector, particularly in export-oriented high-tech activities,[31] where large multinational firms dominate. Why is there a shortage of such entrepreneurs?

There is a well-entrenched view that the dominant role of the government has discouraged private enterprises in many ways. First of all, the presence of well paid public sector jobs has attracted the bright young scholars to the government who could otherwise provide the essential base for domestic entrepreneurship. Secondly, the institutional arrangement of CPF with its high savings rate tends to dampen individual drive for accumulation. Thirdly, the public enterprises are perceived to enjoy certain privileges and advantages over private businesses. Finally, the government's liberal policy towards MNCs has largely 'crowded out' domestic entrepreneurship.

Given the tremendous economic success of Singapore, it is difficult to establish the argument that government intervention, if excessive, can also inhibit economic growth. Serious concerns were however raised about government's over presence[32] in the economy after 1985-86 recession and the issue of public-private mix was hotly debated. The call for privatization also got a fresh momentum at that time and government announced its privatization program in its 1987 report of the divestment committee. Some experts[33] have however claimed that the privatization program will make the role of government even stronger and more extensive. This is because there is an overall budget surplus and so the divestment proceeds are not required to either reduce taxes or expand spending. Instead, these additional funds can be invested at home and abroad. In fact, government enterprises have continued to expand the scope of their activities and their number has also been rising. Thus public sector will continue to play a dominant role in Singapore.

We wish to reiterate that it is not intervention per se but the quality of intervention that matters. With gradual improvements in overall standards of education and training programs, and with stringent criteria of recruitment for civil service--particularly the administrative service, it is likely that the quality of individuals in the government will further be enhanced. Government has also recently revised the salaries of Ministers and civil servants in order to maintain a "continuing flow of man and women of ability and integrity, who will govern the country, mobilize the population, and chart future directions for the nation".[34]

Notes

1   For example, L. B. Krause used the phrase 'economic miracle' in describing the success stories of Singapore and Hongkong in "Hong Kong and Singapore: Twins or Kissing Cousins?", *Economic Development and Cultural Change,* vol. 36, no. 3 (Supplement), 1988, p. 546. The World Bank in its recent publication, *The East Asian Miracle,* New York: Oxford University Press, 1993, included Singapore within "high-performing Asian Economies (HPAEs)" and termed the growth performance of this group (which is comprised of eight countries - Japan, Hong Kong, Republic of Korea, Singapore, Taiwan, Indonesia, Malaysia, and Thailand) as "miraculous" (see p. 1 of the above publication). W.G. Huff, in his most recent review of Singapore's economic performance, *The Economic Growth of Singapore,* Cambridge University Press, Cambridge, 1994, has however suggested that the city-state's economic success, though remarkable, is not a "miracle" for two reasons: First, Singapore started from a high base and second, the international economic forces were extremely favorable to Singapore's growth , see p. 31 in Huff's book.

2   The estimated GDP (at 1985 market prices) in 1993 was S$71,211.9 million, see *Singapore Yearbook of Statistics,* 1994, p. 2, and the actual GDP (based on 1985 market prices) in 1965 was S$6,626.8 million, see *Singapore National Accounts,*1987, p.45.

3   See Ministry of Trade and Industry, *Report of the Economic Committee,* Singapore, February 1986, for details on 1985 recession.

4   Singapore's GNP per capita in 1992 market prices was US$15,730, compared to US$12,210 for Ireland, US$12,300 for New Zealand, and US$13,970 for Spain. For details, see The World Bank, *World Development Report,* 1994, Oxford University Press, London, 1984, p. 163. According to another report, Singapore's per capita GDP in 1993 exceeded that of the United Kingdom. See the Economist Intelligence Unit (EIU), "The World in Figures: Countries" in *The World in 1993,* The Economist Publications, London, 1993), pp. 91-98.

5   See I. Islam, "Political Economy and East Asian Economic Development", *Asian-Pacific Economic Literature,* vol. 6, no. 2, 1992, pp. 69-101 for a near-exhaustive survey of literature on this subject.

6   Singapore's real GDP growth in 1987 was 9.4 percent. See *Singapore Yearbook of Statistics,* 1993, p. 3.

7   Department of Statistics, Singapore, publishes regularly a series on "indigenous per capita GNP" which excludes the foreigners' contribution. This involves the calculation of income accruing to foreign workers and foreign enterprises which are residents of Singapore and the exclusion of this amount from the GNP. The per capita GNP in 1993 was about 20 percent smaller than regular per capita GNP. For details, see *Singapore Yearbook of Statistics,* 1993, p. 2.

8   Small deficits were however reported in 1964 and 1965. For details, see C.Y. Lim and others, *Policy Options for the Singapore Economy,* McGraw Hill, Singapore, 1988, p. 17.

9   A working person in Singapore presently contributes 40 percent of his gross wage to the CPF, with 20 percent from the employee and a further 20 percent from his employer, subject to a certain ceiling. The CPF contribution rates were even higher (50 percent comprised of 25 percent employee's share and 25 percent employer's share) before the 1985-86 economic recession.

10 The public sector savings have taken an increasing share of GNS over time, a significant portion of which are invested overseas by the Government of Singapore Investment Corporation (GIC). For details, see Koh, Ai Tee "Saving, Investment and Entrepreneurship", In L.B. Krause, A.T. Koh, and Y. Lee,

(eds.), *The Singapore Economy Reconsidered,* Institute of Southeast Asian Studies, Singapore, 1987, pp. 78-106.

11 M. Friedman and R. Friedman, 1980, p. 57 in their *Free to Choose* made a similar remark: "Malaysia, Singapore, Korea, Taiwan, Hong Kong and Japan - relying extensively on private markets - are thriving... By contrast, India, Indonesia, and Communist China, all relying heavily on central planning, have experienced economic stagnation".

12 J. Bhagwati in 1988 endorsed such a government intervention in support of his "export promotion (EP)" strategy. An EP strategy is a set of policies which results in the average effective exchange rate for importables being approximately equal to that for exportables.

13 The concept of the developmental state was first put forward by Johnson in 1982 in the context of Japan. In a subsequent contribution (Johnson, 1987) he used the concept 'capitalist developmental state' (or simply the developmental state) to characterize the socio-political structures of Japan, South Korea, and Taiwan. The concept is now firmly entrenched in the development literature and variants of it have been used by others such as Amsden , 1989 and Wade, (1990. For a critical review of the concept, see Z. Onis, "The logic of Developmental State", *Comparative Politics*, October 1991, pp. 109-126.

14 R. Wade, *Governing the Market: Economic Theory and the Role of Government on East Asian Industrialization,* 1990, Princeton University Press, Princeton.

15 A useful distinction is often made in the political science literature between the 'corporatist' and the 'pluralist' regimes. In corporatist system, the state charters or creates a small number of interest groups, giving them a monopoly of representation of occupational interests in return for which it claims the right to monitor them in order to discourage the expression of narrow, conflicting demands. The state is therefore able to shape the demands that are made upon it, and hence maximizes compliance and cooperation. In pluralist regimes, interest groups are voluntary associations, free to organize and gain influence over state policy corresponding to their economic or political resources. The process of government consists of the competition between interest groups, with government bureaucracies playing an important but not generally dominant role. For details, see Zeigler, 1988.

16 G. K. Swee, "A Socialist Economy that Works", in C.V.D. Nair (ed.) *Socialism that Works, The Singapore Way*, Singapore: Federal Publications, 1976, p. 84.

17 O.C. Hock, "The Role of Government in Economic Development: The Singapore Experience", in C.Y. Lim and J.L. Peter (eds.) *Singapore Resources and Growth*, Singapore: Oxford University Press, 1986, p. 234.

18 This conclusion was based on the survey by the Economic Development Board that during 1960-78, the failure rate of the American, Japanese, and European wholly-owned and export-oriented firms was 6.1 percent as compared to 12.8 percent for the wholly-owned foreign firms from other Asian countries such as Hong Kong and Taiwan. See O. C. Hock, 1986, op. cit., p. 235.

19 The education system in Singapore has been tailored accordingly and there are Special Assistance Program (SAP) in certain schools, streaming in primary, secondary, and tertiary levels, special awards for SAF scholars, and so on.

20 Government may not release data on certain sensitive areas. It may also like to withhold some information as it expects from the people a continuance in faith and confidence in its accuracy of judgement and policy formulation based on such privileged data. See C.Y. Lim and others, *Policy Options for the Singapore Economy*, op. cit., 1988, p. 64.

21 The government expenditure to GDP ratio in Singapore is roughly 21 percent which is lower than that in most OECD countries. For details, see The World Bank, *World Development Report*, 1994, Oxford University Press, London, New York.

22 M. G. Asher, "Some Aspects of Role of State in Singapore", *Economic and Political Weekly*, vol. 23, no. 14, April 2, 1994, p. 796.

23 The PAP formed the first government of the State of Singapore in 1959 and since then it has been in power until today.

24 For details on Singapore's labor laws and the implications, see C.H. Tan, "Towards Better Labor-management Relations", In Y.P.Seng and C.Y.Lim (eds.), *Singapore: Twenty-Five Years of Development*, Nanyang Xing Zhou Lianhe Zaobao, 1984.

25 C.H. Wing, Press Secretary to the Prime Minister, "There are Limits to Openness". *The Straits Times*, Thursday, December 29, 1994, p. 26.

26 K.Y. was the Prime Minister of Singapore for more than thirty years, 1959-1990 and presently he is a Senior Minister in G.C. Tong's cabinet. M. Friedman remarked that K.Y.Lee was a 'benevolent dictator' and drew the lesson that "It is Possible to Combine a Free Private Market Economic System with a Dictatorial Political System", cited in W.G. Huff, *The Economic Growth of Singapore*, op. cit., p. 359-360.

27 Government is also quite flexible in its social policies pertaining to education (e.g. graduate mother scheme once introduced for the priority placement in schools of certain categories of children was later withdrawn), population (e.g. change from 'two-child' policy to 'three-child' policy in late 1980s), immigration (e.g. liberal policies introduced in early 1990s to attract foreign talents from the neighboring countries), housing, and so on.

28 In fact, planning in Singapore is based on micro-level project evaluations. Unlike most other countries, Singapore does not have a Five-Year Development Plan. The only available planning document, *First Four-Year Development Plan, 1961-64,* which was prepared under the guidance of the United Nations, was not fully implemented. The setting up of Economic Development Board (EBB) on August 1, 1961 can however be considered the outcome of the Plan as itas strongly recommended by the UN Mission.

29 Currently, the broad economic goals include the attainment of GNP per capita of the United States by 2030 or the Netherlands by 2020. For details, see *The Strategic Economic Plan: Towards a Developed Nation,* Republic of Singapore: Singapore, 1991.

30 Two main types of public enterprises in Singapore are statutory boards and government-linked companies (GLCs). Statutory boards are autonomous organizations set up by specific Acts of Parliament. Almost all infrastructural and public utility services are provided by statutory authorities in Singapore. The activities of the statutory boards are complemented by the GLCs which are in turn owned through three major holding companies. Many GLCs such as Development Bank of Singapore (DBS), Sembawang Group, Keppel Corporation, TDB Holdings, and Singapore Telecoms have been aggressively expanding abroad, often in partnership with domestic and foreign private sector firms. For details, see C.H.Tan, "Public Sector Management: Past Achievement and Future Challenge", In L. Low and M.H. Toh (eds.), *Public Policies in Singapore,* Times Academic Press, Singapore, 1992, pp. 12-29.

31 Singapore's Creative Technology Pte Ltd, which has earned international reputation in the manufacturing of computer chips and sound cards, is perhaps an exception to this observation.

32 It was alleged that the construction sector, which was predominantly under government control, expanded too rapidly leading to a serious glut in the property market. It was also pointed out that the success of state-owned enterprises has been at the expense of private enterprises, and this has led to weakness in the private sector. For details, see C.Y. Lim et al. , 1988. K *Policy Options for the*

Singapore Economy and L.B. Krause, A.T. Koh, and Y. Lee, 1987, *The Singapore Economy Reconsidered,* op. cit.

33 See M.G. Asher, 1994 op. cit. for details on 1987 *Report of the Divestment Committee and its implications for Singapore Economy.*

34 Republic of Singapore, White paper on *Competitive Salaries for Competent and Honest Government,* 1994, p. 1.

References

Amsdem, A., *Asia's Next Giant: South Korea and Late Industrialization,* 1989, Oxford University Press, New York.

Asher, M. G., "Some Aspects of Role of State in Singapore", *Economic and Political Weekly,* 1994, vol. 23, no. 14, April 2. pp. 795-804.

Bhagwati, J., "Export-promoting Trade Strategy: Issues and Evidence", *World Bank Research Observer,* 1988, vol. 3, no. 1, January, pp. 27-57.

Friedman, M. and R. Friedman, *Free To Choose,* 1980, New York: Harcourt Brace Jovanovich.

Goh, K. S., "A Socialist Economy that Works", in C.V. Devan Nair (ed.) *Socialism that Works, The Singapore Way,* 1976, Federal Publications, Singapore.

Huff, W.G., *The Economic Growth of Singapore,* 1994, Cambridge University Press, Cambridge.

Islam, I., "Political Economy and East Asian Economic Development", *Asian-Pacific Economic Literature,* 1992, vol. 6, no. 2, pp. 69-101.

Johnson, C., *MITI and the Japanese Economic Miracle,* 1982, Stanford University Press, Stanford.

Johnson, C., "Political Institutions and Economic Performance: the Government-Business Relations in Japan, South Korea and Taiwan", In Deyo, F. (ed.), *The Political Economy of the New Asian Industrialism,* 1982, Cornell University Press, Ithaca, London.

Krause, L.B., Koh, A.T. and Lee, Y. (eds.), *The Singapore Economy Reconsidered,* 1987, Institute of Southeast Asian Studies, Singapore.

Krause, L. B., "Hong Kong and Singapore: Twins or Kissing Cousins?", *Economic Development and Cultural Change,* 1988, vol. 36, no. 3 (supplement), pp.45-66.

Lim, C.Y. et al., *Policy Options for the Singapore Economy,* 1988, McGraw Hill, Singapore.

Ministry of Trade and Industry, *Report of the Economic Committee,* 1986, Singapore, February.

Onis, Z., "The logic of Developmental State", *Comparative Politics,* 1991, October, pp. 109-126.

Ow, C. H. , "The Role of Government in Economic Development: The Singapore Experience", in Lim Chong Yah and Peter J. Lloyd (eds.) *Singapore Resources and Growth,* 1986, Oxford University Press, Singapore.

Swee, G.K., "A Socialist Economy that Works", in C.V. Devan Nair, ed. *Socialism That Works, the Singapore Way,* 1976, Singapore Federal Publications, p. 84.

Tan, C.H. "Towards Better Labor-management Relations", In Y.P. Seng and Y.C.Lim, (eds.), *Singapore: Twenty-Five Years of Development,* 1984, Nanyang Xing Zhou Lianhe Zaobao, Singapore.

Tan, C. H., "Public Sector Management: Past Achievement and Future Challenge", In L. Low and M.H. Toh (eds.), *Public Policies in Singapore,* 1992, Times Academic Press, Singapore.

Wade, R., *Governing the Market: Economic Theory and the Role of Government on East Asian Industrialization,* 1990, Princeton University Press, Princeton.

The World Bank, *The East Asian Miracle,* 1993, Oxford University Press, New York.

The World Bank, *The World Development Report,* 1994, Oxford University Press, London, New York.

Zeigler, H., *Pluralism, Corporation, and Confucianism: Political Association and Conflict Regulation in the United States, Europe, and Taiwan,* 1988, Temple University Press, Philadelphia.

6 An enduring lesson from Thailand's economic performance

A.T.M. Nurul Amin[1]
Asian Institute of Technology

Abstract

Although the technical details in maintaining macroeconomic stability, rapid expansion of manufacturing exports, attracting foreign investment, promoting market dynamism, and private-public sector cooperation bear many insights for possible emulation by other developing countries seeking economic growth, the chapter argues that the most enduring lesson from Thailand's economic success lies in the arena of political economy that allowed a typical, tropical underdeveloped country with high population growth, the huge underemployment, subsistence agricultural economy, widespread illiteracy, pervasive corruption, perennial political instability, repeated coups and counter coups, authoritarian and dictatorial rule, intermittent and transitory period of failed democratic polity and even armed insurgency--finally to leave all this behind. The political economy lessons are that a technocratic management of an economy for maintaining a continuity of economic policy through swings of political pendulum of democratic strivings and military - autocratic reigns and an early emergence and embracing of a business - enterprise culture, as opposed from a culture of destructive political protests and dissents, are essential for economic growth.

Introduction

Thailand's success in the development effort is undoubtedly remarkable. In less than a decade its income has almost trebled. The per capita income increased from Baht 21,000 in 1986 to Baht 60,000 in 1993. This is clearly the result of GDP growth rate hovering around double digit continuously for the last eight years, whereas, the population growth has continued to decline from 2 percent in 1980 to 1.3 percent in 1993. Thailand is a typical rural-agricultural economy. More than 80 percent of its labor force was engaged in agriculture in 1965 making a contribution of 34.8 percent to the GDP. It is now largely transformed into an urban-industrial economy, leaving only 12 percent of GDP share to the agricultural sector.

Although the employment share of the agricultural sector is still disappointingly[2] high i.e. 67 percent in 1990-92, the economy has already been turned from a labor abundant situation to a labor scarce one with an annual employment growth rate of 4.4 percent during the decade of 1980-90 that includes the recessionary period of 1980-86 which is much higher than the growth rates of population (1.3 percent) as well as labor force (2.2 percent). Overall development is also equally impressive. From 66 in 1991, Thailand climbed to 54 in the Human Development Index (HDI) rank in 1994 among 173 countries of the world that UNDP has been monitoring for reflecting progress by human development criteria, instead of economic growth alone.

This chapter elaborates on the themes and facts touched upon by way of this introduction. It covers the basic facts of economic growth and structural transformation that Thailand has been going through. Bangkok's lead in this transformation and associated spatial imbalances in Thai growth and development are also examined critically in this chapter. It has also assessed the factors that are seen to have made it possible for Thailand to become a leader not only of ASEAN transition but also of positive influence to other developing countries in the larger Asian region if not beyond. The chapter focuses on the doubts, concerns, questions that tend to cloud the Thai success with some concluding remarks.

Performance of the Thai economy

Growth and development

Thailand's economy started to boom from 1987 with nearly double digit growth rates (9.5 percent) that year, followed by 13.3 percent in 1988, 12.2 percent in 1990, 8.4 percent in 1991, 7.9 percent in 1992, 8.2 percent in 1993 and 8.5 percent in 1994. Growth of this order for so many years has naturally made a big impact in Thailand. Whereas this boom has become widely known, what is not clearly known is that this did not come about suddenly. Indeed prior to the beginning of this booming phase, Thailand's economic growth had been remarkably well: 6 percent to 9 percent during 1970-80 and 5.3 percent even during the global recessionary period of 1981-86. The steady growth has thus been sustained for more than two decades. One source of sustaining growth for such a long period and the prospect of its continuation is that all three sectors--agriculture, industry and services--are strong. Equally significant growth has been maintained by all three sectors throughout the last two decades or more. This is clearly shown in Table 6.1.

Whereas the strength of all three economic sectors has put Thailand in a very strongly advantageous footing for long-term sustainability of growth. Indeed, it seems to us that there is no basis in the frequently-heard notion that the Thai economy would

110

Table 6.1
Aggregate and sectoral growth rate in Thailand 1970-92

GDP/Major sector	Year	
	1970-80	1980-92
GDP	7.1	8.2
Agriculture	4.4	4.1
Industry	9.5	10.1
Manufacturing	10.5	10.1
Services	6.8	8.1

Source: The World Bank, *World Development Report,* 1994, Oxford University Press , p.165.

collapse if tourism and the associated entertainment services would falter. The rapid growth of manufacturing reaching a level of 28 percent of GDP (industrial sectors's overall share is nearly 40 percent) is one manifestation of its clear transition to the NIE (newly industrialized economy) status.

Structural transformation

In line with steady economic growth of more than two decades, topped with the boom, remarkable structural transformation has been underway in Thailand for quite some time. Although space consideration requires the focus here to be limited to structural transformation of economic dimensions, it is to be noted that the changes in the basic economic structure as depicted in Table 6.2 has been associated with (as always is the case) profoundly significant change in political and social structures as well as in cultural, attitudinal and behaviourial aspects.[3]

Most remarkable is a more than threefold drop of agricultures's share to GDP, and doubling of the industrial sector's contribution during the same period from 18.6 percent in 1960 to 39.2 percent in 1990. While the importance of agriculture continues to diminish, its share of work force is still high: 66.5 percent. Although one is not certain of the accuracy (because of widespread presence of mixed occupations, classification of the rural labor force is complex[4]) of this high figure, such a huge proportion of labor turning in only 12 percent of GDP obviously denotes a productivity problem for the agricultural sector. But even on this perennial problem the booming economy has made an impact: in just three years the average agricultural productivity rose from 10.15 in 1986 to 17.06 in 1991.[5]

The industrial sector scenario is much brighter. Not only the sector as a whole has been rapidly expanding as evident in the doubling of its GDP share, more happily the manufacturing part continues to make greater strides: from 16 percent in 1970, its GDP share rose to 28 percent in 1992. Productivity of manufacturing is also very

111

Table 6.2
Structural transformation in Thailand 1960-90

Year	Sectoral share of GDP			Population distribution		Work force by sector	
	Agr.	Ind.	Serv.	Rural	Urban	Agr.	Non-agr.
1960	39.8	18.6	41.7	–	–	–	–
1970	25.9	25.3	48.8	86.7	13.3	78.9	21.2
1980	23.2	31.0	45.8	82.7	17.3	71.0	29.0
1990	12.4	39.2	48.4	77.4	22.6	66.5	33.5

Source: Muscat, 1994, p. 293, ESCAP 1993, pp. 2-11, and H. Utaserani and Yongkittikul 1993, p. 138 respectively for data on sectoral share of GDP, rural-urban distribution of population, and employment by agricultural and non-agricultural sectors.

impressive: this 28 percent of GDP comes from 11 percent of the total work force. This is suggestive of an employment problem. Fortunately that has not been the case: overall employment generation (particularly in the service, construction, housing, infrastructure sectors) has rather created a tight labor market situation--a feat that seems so impossible today for most countries. Growth dynamism of the manufacturing sector is reflected more in the composition change of exports as shown in Table 6.3.

Overall, a total reversal of Thailand's status as a primary goods producer and exporter has taken place in two decades. Two pieces of evidence illustrate this very strikingly. One, as seen before (Table 6.2), in 1960 the share of agriculture to GDP

Table 6.3
Change in the structure of exports 1970-92

Type of exports	Year	
	1970	1992
Fuel, mineral, metals	15	2
Other primary commodities	77	21
Machinery and transport equipment	0	22
Other manufactures	8	45
Textiles, clothing	1	17

Source: The World Bank, *The World Development Report*, 1994, Oxford University Press, London p. 191.

was 39.8, whereas in 1990 the order of that magnitude (to be precise 39.2 percent) is taken over by the industrial sector. Two, in 1970 the share of primary commodities (other than fuels, minerals and metal) stood at 77 percent, whereas in 1992 a similarly high proportion (67 percent) of exports comprised manufacturing goods (Table 6.3). This is clearly a remarkable feat of achievement by any historical precedence.

The shift of human settlements from rural to urban area is an important dimension of socio-economic transformation. The level of urbanization, measured by the proportion of total population living in urban area, shows change in human settlements pattern. Thailand has been a typical rural-agricultural economy for ages like most other developing countries. Even in 1970 nearly 86.7 percent of Thai people lived in rural area. In 1990 this proportion dropped to 77.4 percent as shown in Table 6.2. Some sources show a larger drop in rural population. At any rate, our best approximation is that about one-third of Thai people now live in urban area. More importantly, the trend is of rapid increase: during 1970-1990, the growth rate has been 5.0 percent per annum. This pace is an indication that a more congruent relationship between economic development and urbanization will soon get established in Thailand too. According to the historical relationship observed among a large cross-section of countries over a long period of time, Thailand's predicted value of urban share in total population is in the order of 40 percent. That is to say: at the current per capita income level, 40 percent of Thai people were to be expected to live in urban areas. The actual figure by all estimates is much lower (about 23 percent).

There are many plausible explanations of this. Strong cultural attachment of the people to rural land and living is one. The hypothesis that we have offered is that it is due to the highly skewed urban structure of Thailand. The urban hierarchy of Thailand is overwhelmingly dominated by a single city: Bangkok. The primacy of Bangkok is exceedingly high, whatever is the measure used. Absence of regional countermagnate or large regional cities have made rural to urban migration virtually a one-city bound destination. This situation has naturally constrained overall urban absorption. It is the current economic boom, although its Bangkok-centeredness limits the potential, coupled with continuation of planned urban decentralization[6] that should finally bring a balanced urban structure in Thailand.

Urban development

Our scrutiny of labor force survey data of Thailand for the last two decades suggest significant change in the employment structure of Thailand. Since change in the Thai labor force engaged in agriculture and non-agricultural occupations was already shown (Table 6.2), here we limit attention to the urban employment structure. Distribution of urban employed labor by work status described in Table 6.4 shows a substantial rise in 'private employee' category which denote the employees employed by the private sector. This reflects a large increase in wage and salary earners in the economy as opposed to those who are self-employed. Evidence on the latter is seen in the data

Table 6.4

Percentage distribution of employed persons in the municipal areas of Thailand by work status 1976-88

Year			Work status percent			
	Employer	Government employee	Private employee worker	Own account worker	Unpaid family	Estimated size of in formal sector
1976	1.8	17.5	37.9	28.9	13.9	65.2
1980	3.4	16.1	42.6	22.8	15.0	62.9
1988	4.4	17.8	45.3	19.7	12.7	59.1

Source: Based on the respective year's *Labor Force Survey Report* , July-September round. Amin , 1994:62 contains data for each year of 1976 to 1988.
*Private employee x 59% + (Own account worker) + (Unpaid family worker).

on 'own account workers' and 'unpaid family labor'. As can be seen from Table 6.4, in 1976 these two groups together accounted for 42.8 percent of urban work force in Thailand. By 1988 this has declined to 32.4 percent. In contrast, the proportion of 'private employees' (i.e. wage and salary earners in the private sector alone) rose from 37.9 percent to 45.3 percent. Our estimate for the informal sector employment also shows a decline: from 65.2 percent in 1976 to 59.1 percent in 1988. This large increase in wage & salary earners and substantial reduction in informal sector size are clear outcomes of rapid economic growth in Thailand.

In view of the dominance of Bangkok in the urban structure of Thailand, Amin[7] examines similar data of even longer period. These data suggest that the Thai economic growth has altered the size as well as content of Bangkok's informal sector. While substantially reducing the fold of marginal occupations, economic growth has spurred expansion of the dynamic and entrepreneurial component of the informal sector. This is evident in the remarkable reduction of the share of 'own account workers' (i.e., petty trader and service activities of one-person operation) and 'unpaid family workers' (who assist the informal sector family enterprises) in Bangkok's working labor force. These two labor categories together accounted for 33.3 percent of the total working labor in 1971, which got reduced to 28.7 percent in 1980. By 1993, their share further declined to 23.9 percent. In contrast, the dynamic informal enterprises (which employ some wage/hired labor, in addition to the 'owner-operators' or 'own-account workers' or 'unpaid family workers', as commonly observed in production of garments, leather goods, toys, metal products, artificial flowers, processed food, jewellery, furniture, etc.) expanded from a share of 26.8 percent of total Bangkok employment in 1971 to 31.4 percent in 1980 and 33.8 percent in 1993. This is a remarkable trend showing the impact of steady economic growth of the last two decades and the boom of recent years (since 1987). On the whole, the sector declined from employing 60.1 percent of the total Bangkok labor in 1980 to 57.7 percent in 1993.[8]

Rural and agricultural development

The writings of two distinguished Thai scholars Ammar Siamwalla and Phisit Pakkasem[9] suggest profoundly significant change in Thai rural economy too. The latter, a leading figure in the Thai development planning of the recent years as a chief executive of the National Economic and Social Development Board (NESDB) until 1994, in his very topically valuable book, *Leading Issues in Thailand's Development Transformation* 1960-1990, authoritatively describes major features of spatial-sectoral transformation in Thailand. In this, the rural-agricultural transformation features are traced to the (a) green revolution impacts that have been underway since the mid-sixties and (b) rural hinterland impacts of the mostly Bangkok-centered urban-industrial transformation that has been underway for sometime gaining a momentum from the recent economic boom.

Although the "spatial" transformation from the green revolution is characterized as limited, Pakkasem[10] carefully outlines the immediate impacts of the water-seeds-fertilizer technology that came as a package of the green revolution. Within two years of its introduction, cropping intensity increased by 85 percent (from 1966 to 1968) and cropping pattern changed "drastically" with more switching to transplanting than broadcasting that resulted doubling of labor hiring by big farmers. By 1976 (a) high-yielding seeds accounted for 40 percent of the total wet season crop, (b) yield increased by 20 to 30 percent and (c) two-thirds of area came under tractor use. Mechanization spread rapidly for land preparation, transport, and threshing as a result of the introduction of double cropping and land consolidation. Fertilizer use rose steadily. Institutional credit accessibility remained limited: less than half of the farmers and usually the larger ones could avail such credit. Pakkasem[11] concludes that rural transformation impacts of green revolution basically consists of: increase use of modern inputs and technology on the parts of those who could make investment for higher yield and returns and (b) widening of income disparities between land consolidated/irrigated area farmers and rainfed area farmers. He, however, adds that despite their disadvantages, the small farmers did participate in green revolution and fared well.

On rural hinterlands impacts of urban-industrial transformation, Pakkasem-reported results may be summarized as follows.[12] One, the households of Bangkok-close locations (the hypothesis is that these areas will gain more from spread effects of Bangkok-centered urban-industrial transformation) did not experience significantly different impact in terms of the structure of agriculture (specifically in agriculture diversification) than those of the far-off locations. However, increased commercialization of agriculture was found in both types of areas which is considered an impact of urban-industrial transformation; two, the cost structure of farming changed in the Bangkok-proximate areas for greater dependence on modern inputs and their higher costs. Three, the non-farm income increase accrued to the Bangkok-proximate area households appear as the most tangible impact. Four, the more striking has been the change in consumption habits of residents in these locations due to demonstration effects. Five, wages were higher in these 'metro-shadow' locations than the out-lying areas but this did not make the propensity of migration different: both sub-region (i.e., close and far-off) residents were equally motivated to a Bangkok-ward migration. Six, about 24 to 26 percent of households (of the two combined group) received remittances from members residing in Bangkok; of whom 75 percent reported remittances to families in rural areas. Pakkasem[13] observes that urban-industrial transformation has had both spread and backwash effects on the rural hinterland: some benefits radiate into the shadow subregion but resources are drawn out of the hinterland as well.

The most resourceful source on rural-agricultural transformation in Thailand is Siamwalla,[14] the chief executive of the prestigious research institution -- Thailand Development Research Institute (TDRI). Although in his popular writings, he often expresses concern on "rural-urban divide", the overall scenario he depicts in his scholarly writings is one of clear optimism. For example, the broadening of the "manufacturing base", he observes, "will ease the pressure on the forest cover after four decades of continual land expansion". He expects "the absolute size of the (permanent) agricultural labor force will shrink sometime during the 1990s", which will lead to lowering the demand for labor. An all round positive scenario including environmental improvement is thus predicted as a result of urban-industrial led economic growth and development that has been sweeping Thailand.

Imbalances in the development process

Bangkok's pre-eminence

It will be no exaggeration to say that Thailand's economic, political and social transformation is a history of Bangkok's transformation. As detailed below in the text and in Table 6.5, the facts on Bangkok's primacy in the urban-industrial economy of Thailand is truly overwhelming. Our basic contention, however, is that in the on-going economic boom, and the accompanying structural change in Thailand, Bangkok is affecting the whole fabric of Thai society and its economic life too. Of course it itself is getting changed almost beyond recognition with an increasing number of high rises, fly-overs, expressways, numerous cars and eye-dazzling department stores. Completion of the recently undertaken huge infrastructural projects of mass transits, expressways, skytrain, road network will soon change the face of Bangkok further. Yet Bangkok, we contend, is very much rooted to Thai soil, people and culture. It does not strike as a city superimposed from outside through the process of colonial and neo-colonial links as is the case with many third world cities. It is very much a Thai city. Maybe the presence of the informal sector people along the city streets and sois (lanes) with overcrowded vending of locally made food, goods (imported as well as their local counterfeits) and their slum living with continued contacts with rural kins have helped to preserve the Thai character and culture in Bangkok. Bangkok-centered economic growth and modernity instead of destroying the Thai culture schemes to have enriched it.

All commonly used measures point to an extraordinary level of primacy for Bangkok. This has been the case throughout despite some planning efforts to alter this. From 45 percent in 1947, Bangkok's share of national urban population rose to a staggering height of 69 percent in the eighties as seen in Table 6.5. Since then the share seems to have dropped (57 percent in 1990), although the growth is still much higher than the national average. The BMR population grew at 2.5 percent per annum during 1986-2001, the projected growth is still similar: 2.3 percent compared to 1.4 percent of Thailand.

That Bangkok's population is 50 times that of the next most populous city, Nakohn Ratchasima, further illustrates the single-city dominance of Thailand's urban structure. The four-city primacy index comparison of cities in Asia-Pacific region confirms this peculiarity in Thailand's urban development. Even compared to similar large city dominant countries (e.g. Indonesia, Philippines, Korea) Thailand is hugely different as illustrated in their four-city index values Bangkok (16.35), Seoul (1.43), Jakarta (1.33) and Manila (1.13).

Hand in hand with demographic preponderance, Bangkok accounts for large part of Thailand's GDP (44 percent), industrial output (77 percent), and infrastructural investments (60 percent)as seen in Table 6.6. Unlike some drop in the share of population, there is no sign yet of any decline in Bangkok's share in vital investment, output, and consumption. Ratanakomut, Ashakul and Krinanda[15] report that "the BMR accounted for almost 70 percent of total value added in manufacturing between

Table 6.5
Trend in Bangkok's primacy status

Year	Bangkok's share of Thailand's urban population
1947	45
1960	52
1969	60
1977	65
1980	69
1990	57

Source: Pakkasem , 1988, p. 32, Mills, 1989, p. 3, and *World Development Report*, 1994, p. 223 respectively for data of 1947-77, 1980, and 1990.

Table 6.6
Bangkok's primacy in Thailand's economy

Index	Percent
Share of national urban population	69
Share of GDP	36
Share of industrial production	41
Share of national infrastructural investments	60

Source: Mills, 1989, p. 3 for item 1: Pakkasem, 1988, p. 86 for item 2 & 3; and Richardson, 1984, pp. 110-111.

1981 and 1988. Twelve of the country's 23 industrial estates were within its confines". The Board of Investment (BOT) data purportedly show that the BMR's five inner provinces attracted the bulk of BOT approved projects. They also note BMR's status as the biggest consumer market of over 9 million people for durable and nondurable goods and as the hub of best social infrastructures (e.g. piped water, telephones, hospitals, and leisure facilities).

Consequent imbalances

A variety of urban problems (e.g. a total stalemate in traffic movement, serious air and water pollution) are almost crippling Bangkok economically and quality of life-wise as infrastructural investment growth lagged behind the pace of demographic and economic growth as a result of the boom. To alleviate this situation and to improve urban productivity and quality of life, which have been part of the guiding principles of the Seventh Plan, huge infrastructural projects are now underway. One issue here is if these urban problems were not to be considered as exhaustion of scale and agglomeration economies or if these huge investments will not further deteriorate the spatial imbalances in Thailand and simultaneously reinforce segmentation in urban economy and living environment even within Bangkok (i.e., more capital consuming, technologically sophisticated production and affluent living versus continuation of the low-productive informal sector and slum living).

Although our monitoring of income, employment and housing data[16] suggest steady decline in growth of the informal sector and slums, there is a real danger of over investment in Bangkok in a pattern that may reverse this process. Several factors have created a favorable mood for undertaking huge infrastructural investment without proper efficiency and equity considerations. One of these factors is the "failure" to arrest the growth of Bangkok through the regional and secondary city development projects of the fifth and sixth plan. Indeed a large number of externally funded technical assistance projects were undertaken to assist creation of a regional urban sector--a decentralized urban system. The review of those projects and experiences of fifth and sixth plans have led to a view as if nothing much can be done to slow down Bangkok's growth. Two, the concern for productivity loss due to traffic congestion and other urban problems is another important factor. Three, the prevailing global economic and political mood against distributive policies have also influenced the shelving of urban decentralization in Thailand in favor of Bangkok.

Imbalance weakening trends

Thailand's structural imbalances, whether it is rural-urban divide or Bangkok's overwhelming primacy or regional disparities or concentration of wealth, have historical roots (e.g. the 'sakdina' system that rationalized the hierarchical order; the long persistence of peasant economy made possible by the availability of land; and the resource-base variability among the four distinct natural eco-region of the country) as much as they are the outcome of modern development process.

Nonetheless, the phase has clearly started when economic growth weakens structural imbalances of all forms. The study of 1962-86 period by Ikemoto,[17] a thoroughly objective and comprehensive work, already revealed improving signs in interregional as well as interpersonal income distribution. Our hypothesis is that this trend has continued since then. The compiled evidence of Table 6.7 provides strong basis for the hypothesis. Five measures -- Bangkok's primacy, urban-rural income ratio, interregional income ratio, Gini Coefficient and population below poverty line-- all point to a gradual decline in the imbalances that have been so much part of Thai economic and social history. A remarkable piece of evidence in these data is that: the only time period when the declining trend has not been maintained is that of 1980-86 --the global recessionary period that also slowed down Thailand's economy. This may be seen as an indirect support to the basic point that we are making: imbalances, inequalities and incidence of poverty is getting reduced in Thailand through economic growth.

In view of the above data, it is no surprise that Thailand is placed today among the seven "high-growth, low-inequality economies" of the world--all belonging to the East Asia. Although Thailand is at the bottom of these seven, it is holding a position that is so much better than most other developing countries.

Two qualifications seem to be in order here. One, the point made above should not be construed to imply that economic growth *per se* automatically lowers imbalances and inequalities. What it does is: it generates social and political forces that force policy and planning actions for distributive justice. In case of Thailand it is remarkably illustrated by two historical episodes: one, the October 1973 student uprising preceded by steady economic growth that culminated into the 1973-76 democracy period coinciding with an improvement in income distribution; two, the May 1992 anti-military uprising preceded by the ushering in of economic boom that

Table 6.7
Trend in inequalities and poverty in Thailand

Variable	Year					
	1960	1970	1975	1980	1985	1990
Bangkok' primacy: proportion of total urban population (%)	52	65	–	69	–	57
Income ratio of urban rural areas	–	2.73 (1969)	2.27	2.09 (1981)	2.25 (1986)	–
Income ratio of region with highest to the lowest per capita household income	4.7 (1962)	3.38 (1969)	2.43	2.25 (1981)	2.86 (1986)	–
Gini co-efficient	0.413 (1962)	0.426 (1969)	0.417	0.441 (1981)	0.471 (1986)	0.465 (1988)
Proportion of population below poverty line (%)	59.0 (1962)	–	30.0	23.0 (1981)	29.5 (1986)	22.8 (1988)

Source: Item 1 sources are noted in Table 6.5. For items 2 , 3 and 4 Ikemoto, 1991, pp. 60,11 except Gini of 1988 which is from Rattanakomut, Ashakul and Kirandana , 1994, p. 205; and item 5 from Muscat, 1994, p. 243 except the figure for 1962 which is from World Bank, 1993.

culminated in election of the present democratic government with commitment to reduce rural-urban disparities and improve distributive justice.

Yet, Thailand has still a long way to go to reverse the still unacceptable level of inequities as manifested in the fact that the lowest 20 percent of the population share only 6.1 percent of total income, whereas, the corresponding shares of the highest 20 percent is 50.7 percent.

What made it possible?

Japanese investment

Direct foreign investment (DFI), particularly that of Japan has been a crucial factor in the growth that is now sweeping the ASEAN region. The World Bank[18] highlights DFI's role in spurring Thailand's exports. Guillouet[19] provides data showing growing importance of Japan in the region as a result of rapid increase in investment in manufacturing, physical infrastructures, financial sector and human capital development. Data from government sources data show that from 23 percent of total DFI in 1980, Japanese investment soared to 52 percent by 1988. Even golf course has become a field of Japanese investment. The popular perception is that the Japanese have also been buying Thai land in large scale. Most Thais, however, seem to consider the Japanese investment as a singularly important external factor for their economic boom. It seems to have served a "big push" role for the Thai economy. The traditional close economic relations between Japan and Thailand got new impetus from relocation of many Japanese production facilities as a result of increase in production costs in Japan and continuous appreciation of yen value.

Since 1988, Thailand replaced Indonesia as the primary recipient of Japanese investment in the ASEAN countries. Thai-Japanese economic relations has been working without any hiss. Some resentment that prevailed against Japanese products in the early seventies have disappeared since then. The benefits of jobs, technology and gains from exports outweigh perceived or any real negative effects. Of course the strategic switch from Japanese products importing to attracting investment has made the economic relations all this different.

Investment from other countries

Thailand has also been benefiting from investment by other East Asian miracle economies. Appreciation of the Korean won and the Taiwanese dollar led to a surge of investment from these two countries too.

Whereas the investments from these sources made a large and rapid impact in the recent years, the long-prevailing political and economic relations with the West, particularly the U.S. prepared Thailand well for increasing its investment absorptive capacity. Circumstances centering World War II, Korean War and particularly the Vietnam War placed Thailand in an advantageous position to receive U.S. investments in defense, infrastructures, manpower training and direct expenditures by U.S. military and civil personnel stationed in the region. Muscat[20] highlights this aspect with a chronology of U.S.-Thailand relations and their corresponding gains accrued to the Thai economy.

Technocratic management

Analysts give credit to the role of technocrats for Thailand's development policies since the mid-1950s. In several instances the technocrats were placed in key positions by the authoritarian or military dictators but their competence and critical mind served the national and people's cause well. The most recent example of this was the installation of Anand Panyarachum as the Prime Minister with the February 1991 military coup that overthrew an elected government. Anand succeeded to bring a group of technocrats in the cabinet that served the country's economic interests very well. Simultaneously, Anand remained loyal to the democratic aspirations of the political forces in the country without caring much about the coup leaders who installed him.

The most illustrious role of early technocratic leadership with firm commitment to the interest of people came from Dr. Puey Ungphakorn, a graduate of London School of Economics of early fifties, who as the Director of the Budget Bureau, as one of the long-serving governor of central bank, and as rector of Thammasat University until the rightist insurgency of October 1976 inspired and influenced a breed of young western-trained professionals holding key economic policy making positions in the central bank, the Ministry of Finance, NESDB, and the Budget Bureau. As Muscat[21] depicts, this way Dr. Puey's reputation helped to establish, from early on, a core group of professional technocrats in the charge of financial control and development policy-making and create the institutional basis of its continuation.

The 1991 World Bank-IMF annual meeting was ostentiously held in Bangkok to give recognition to efficient macroeconomic management of Thailand that is seen to have paved the way for its economic success. Thailand is credited as one of the few developing countries which "have managed to keep their macroeconomic policies on course."[22] Its broad economic performance has benefitted accordingly.

Continuity of economic policy

Despite Thailand never being a country of political stability, it is perhaps the best illustration among developing countries of economic policy continuity. The basic economic policy framework of Thailand has remained mostly undisturbed under political instability, uncertainty, coups and counter coups, violence, and even insurgencies. Muscat[23] observes that Thailand has manifested its ability to turn to its central long-term policy tendency from one regime to another.

Flexibility and compromising attitudes of Thai people and the role of the long-reigning current Monarch, Ram IX (King Bhumibol Adulyadez since June 1946), as an anchor of stability have served Thailand very well in providing a long-term stability that is so distressingly lacking in most developing countries. Perhaps this is one of the most enduring lesson from Thai success. A country does not need a monarchic system for this essential stability and continuity. A national consensus on long-term economic framework can provide policy continuity through political and government changes.

Rapid growth of manufacturing

Thailand proves again that without a shift from overwhelming reliance on traditional agricultural economy, no country can become prosperous. This is simply because the odds are too many against rural-agricultural products, albeit they include the basic of all basic needs i.e. food. Elsewhere we have shown that their low income and price elasticities, unfavorable terms of trade, perfectly competitive market conditions, limited scope of benefiting from scale and agglomeration economies, absence of much technological innovation and capital accumulation (vis-à-vis their urban-industrial counterparts) place a predominantly primary goods producing and exporting economy in a structural disadvantage. Thailand overcame this disadvantage steadily as development planning progressed. From a natural-resource based export regime of 1955-70, Thailand moved to a regime of supporting import substitution during 1971-80, followed by manufacturing for exports from 1980 which has been continuing since then with remarkable success.

Rapid demographic transition

From 3.3 percent in 1960, Thailand succeeded to bring down the population growth rate below 2.0 percent per annum by the mid-eighties. This has now dropped to 1.3 percent. No country of this level of development has been able to bring down the population growth so dramatically. In addition to planning efforts, cultural, education and economic factors made this possible. Muscat considers that "the economic and material conditions of rural life, which began to change rapidly in the 1960s, preceded and largely precipitated the change in family-size preference."[24] Both government and non-government organizations (e.g. the campaign of the Population Development Association (PDA) for its innovative use of humor that has earned its President, Meechai Ruchupan, the title of Condom Man/King) gained international recognition for successful campaign to reduce population growth. Consequently, the per capita investment has been higher in Thailand compared to most other developing countries whose all development efforts and gains get lost to population growth that still exceeds more than two percent.

High women participation in the labor force

Unlike most other developing countries, women participation in labor force is very high i.e. 47 percent in 1990 in Thailand. For international media coverage of women in the entertainment industry, the role of hard-working Thai women engaged in numerous low-keyed informal and formal occupations (specially in the sales, service and manufacturing geared to exports) remains largely unrecognized. Phongpaichit[25] sheds some light on women's vast and enterprising role in subcontracting and piece-rate work involving exports of garments, textiles, leather products, artificial flowers, gem stones, etc.

Business enterprise culture

Although the majority of Thai comes of rural origin, the strong presence of urban-centered Chinese ethnic group provided the initial nucleus of an enterprising business culture that soon spread to the mainstream Thais. Unlike the situation in South Asian

123

countries, political-intellectual non-business orientation of the elites never commanded much interest and prestige among the masses of Thai people.

Muscat[26] traces the enterprise culture in Thailand to the Thais of Chinese origin. Whereas availability of such special group to foster enterprise culture is a special situation, promotion of business-industrial culture in any country is possible if intellectual and political elites grasp its significance for economic prosperity.

Land abundance and strong agricultural sector

Land abundance has not been a small factor in defining the nature and pattern of Thailand's economic growth and development. Whereas this does not obviously offer any policy lesson for others, the strong agriculture (which has been acquired through conscious efforts and prudent policies) does. The World Bank[27] analysis shows all HPAEs, particularly Thailand, are characterized by "strong and dynamic agriculture". This does not necessarily undermine the previous point on the role of manufacturing in Thailand's transformation as a NIE. Indeed the two sectors have complemented one another in each growing stronger. The point made earlier is that it is only at the phase of rapid growth of manufacturing that the real breakthrough occurred. Initial conditions of land abundance and never being a food deficit country placed Thailand in an advantage. What it achieved through policy and planning is successful implementation of the green revolution package and making agro-processing industries a centerpiece of manufacturing.

Doubts, questions, concerns

Despite the success (acclaimed by most analysts including institutions of the World Bank and IMF's stature) and the associated pride and pleasure of Thai people, souring of it comes from varied quarters. The NGO (Non-government Organization) circles have been particularly vocal in this for damage to the country's natural environment and cultural values of the Thai people. Media coverage of NGO activists and Bangkok-centeredness of the growth often make headlines. For example, a 1994 cover story in the Far Eastern Economic Review is captioned as *Thailand: Separate and Unequal*. Then it goes on to say (with prominent display):

> With most of its booming industry concentrated around Bangkok, Thailand is in danger of becoming two nations: one urbanized and wealthy, the other rural and impoverished.[28]

Some academic writings, based on field research, also express concerns. For example, Atkinson and Vorratnchaiphan lament erosion of valued Thai culture and natural living environment. Environmental damage also fairs in Douglass and

Zoghlin [29] "although economic growth has propelled the Thai economy to the brink of being a real 'newly industrialized country', the environment continues to suffer greatly in its path". Expressing similar concern for the poor, they claim that whatever wage increases occurred from economic boom did not bore benefits to the urban poor because of higher land prices. It does not seem that this claim can be borne out by data. The employment and housing data of Bangkok for nearly two decades (1971-1993) show: (a) an unambiguous decline in marginal occupations in the informal sector, (b) a substantial drop in slum housing, and (c) a much higher rise in minimum wages compared to the inflationary rate in the economy. We take this as strong evidence of benefits accruing to the urban poor from the Thai economic growth and prosperity. Since urban poverty to a large extent is a transfer of rural poverty in economy with large rural population (as it is the case in Thailand), those findings imply overall improvement in poor's employment, income and housing conditions.

A careful reading of various viewpoints on recent changes in Thailand strikingly reveal two differing perspectives. In one, people's welfare is seen to advance from better employment, higher income, improved housing and other material conditions as in this instance has been afforded by Thailand's rapid economic growth in recent years. In the other, the new paradigms of development such as 'people's participation', 'community development', 'ecologically and environmentally sustainable development', etc. dominate as means as well as measure of people's welfare. In the latter perspective any economic growth, development planning, market dynamism-based success story is of suspect as it is in the case of Thailand and hence castigated.

At any rate, whatever may be the intellectual or ideological orientation, all critiques need to be understood and addressed. To everybody's benefit Muscat [30] has very authoritatively, objectively and comprehensively addressed these lingering doubts, questions and concerns grouping them under five headings: (1) export pessimism, (2) environment and natural resources, (3) fairness and balance, (4) structural imbalances, and (5) corporate concentration. [31] Some of these issues have already faired in our discussion. Although we cannot have a focussed discussion on each of these five issues, it seems fair to say that the overall assessment of Muscat is firmly optimistic. His optimism is based on as he says "on the record of the past three decades and ... in a continuing balance of *growth, stability,* and *equity*" (emphasis added) [32] as Thailand reflects today. Such a balancing will take care of the well-meaning concerns that tend to cloud a truly outstanding success.

Concluding remarks

Starting from a largely autarkic subsistence economy, overwhelmingly agricultural and hardly penetrated by science and technology or industry, Thailand has been slowly modernizing for nearly a century. [33]

This passage is quoted here to make two key points that we had thought of making in this concluding section. The first one is to state the profoundness of the transformation: that subsistence, autarkic, agricultural economy is now an urban-industrial-service economy (note that this service is increasingly of higher-order service, at least in Bangkok, as recently noted by Kaothien and Webster:[34] "The economy of Bangkok's core is changing rapidly. Knowledge based activity is growing fast ..."). Indeed, "The stage is long past when Thailand was simply a pleasant agricultural country."[35]

The second point is that this transformation has not been as dramatic or rapid or miraculous as now projected. Those who know Thailand only by the on-going economic boom that has been sweeping since 1987 could arrive at such an erroneous conclusion. Muscat[36] notes efforts of nearly a century. If that is stretching too much, three decades of planned efforts are clearly on record as reflected in the data presented previously that gradually resulted the sectoral transformation encompassing production, employment, and rural-urban distribution of population. Thus, what has been underway at least for last three decades cannot be characterized as miraculous or rapid and dramatic resulting from a boom. As a matter of fact, in 1988, just the second year of the on-going boom, transformation of Thailand from a rural-agricultural-resource base to an urban-industrial-service economy was already noted by Pakkasem.[37] Obviously such structural transformation of this nature cannot result from economic growth of one or two years however high that growth rate may be and that also just after the economy coming out of a grueling recession that ended only in 1986.

The reason we are laboring to make these two inter-related points is to really make a third point, which we consider important for countries curious to learn from Thailand's experience. This is a simple point: There is no miraculous or short-cut way to economic progress. The course is long and an arduous one. Many query this author: "How could Thailand make it? After all Thailand has not been much different than us", etc. Typical developing country problems--high population growth, huge underemployment, subsistence agricultural economy, widespread illiteracy, pervasive corruption, perennial political instability, repeated coups and counter-coups, authoritarian and dictatorial rule, intermittent and transitory period of failed democratic polity, even armed insurgency, etc.--have truly been, at one stage or another, Thailand's problems too. Even today it is not free from all of these legacies. Here lies the significance of Thailand's success, which has been attained despite having all the contemporary attributes of underdevelopment (except the colonial legacy). To our mind the key lessons from Thailand's success are: one, continuous striving is essential for economic growth; two, no negative image or characteristic can keep an economy backward for ever; three, economic growth alone can set the social and political forces in motion that ultimately ensure distributive justice, better quality of life and living environment (not the other way round).

Although technical details in (a) maintaining macroeconomic stability, (b) rapid expansion of manufacturing exports, (c) attracting foreign investment, (d) promoting market dynamism, and (e) private-public sector cooperation bear many insights for possible emulation by other developing countries seeking economic growth, it seems to us that the most enduring lesson from Thailand's success is that of political economy dimension as indicated above. Thus, it is no surprise that Thailand has become a source of inspiration for change beyond its ASEAN partners. It has already helped to transform the Indo-Chinese "battlefield into a trading zone". Thailand has been influencing Myanmar's gradual opening up too. The South Asian countries are courting Thailand for possible cooperation between SAARC[38] and ASEAN. All of this, and potentially more, is a direct fallout of Thailand not being too remote, not being a miracle; and it being a tropical and typical developing economy.

Notes

1   The author would like to express his gratitude to professor H. Kazi, Director, United Nations Center for Regional Development (UNCRD) Nagoya, Japan for inviting him under a United Nations Fellowship to utilize his sabbatical leave from the Asian Institute of Technology (AIT), Bangkok, Thailand that allowed him writing this chapter among other things.

2   Disappointing because 67 percent of total labor force turning in only 12 percent of GDP obviously denote a productivity problem.

3   This author has been a witness of these changes since 1987 when the boom started. Some documented sources are : Muscat, 1994 for economic and political development; Atkinson and Vorratnchaiphan, 1994 for concerns on social, cultural and environmental changes that have accompanied Thailand's development; and Korff , 1986 for sociological analysis of Bangkok's social and economic system (focused on slums and until the boom time).

4   Muscat, 1994 points out methodological problem that may have overstated the size of agricultural labor force.

5   Author's calculation based on NSO, 1993 data.

6   A. Amin, "Bangkok's Informal Sector and Slums Through the Thai Economic Growth and Prosperity", chapter presented at the International Seminar on *Human Settlements Problems in Metropolitan Core Areas*, 1995-b, Tokyo.

7   Ibid.

8   A. Siamwalla, "Land Abundant Agricultural Growth and Some of Its Consequences: The Case of Thailand", 1990, Bangkok, TDRI; and P. Pakkasem, *Leading Issues in Thailand's Development Transformation*, 1988, Bangkok: National Economic and Social Development Board.

9 P. Pakkasem, 1988, op. cit.

10 Ibid.

11 Ibid. pp 34-37.

12 Ibid.

13 Ibid.

14 A. Siamwalla, 1990, op. cit.

15 S. Ratanakomut, C. Ashakul and T. Krinanda, "Urban Poverty in Thailand: Critical Issues and Policy Measures", *Asian Development Review*, 1994, vol. 12, no. 1.

16 A. Amin, 1995-b, op. cit.

17 Y. Ikemoto, *Income Distribution, Its Changes, Causes and Structure*, 1991, Tokyo, Institute of Developing Economies.

18 The World Bank, *The East Asian Miracle: Economic Growth and Public Policy*, 1993, Washington, D.C.

19 A. Guillouet, *Booming Economics of South East Asia: Thailand, Malaysia, Singapore*, 1990, Longman Singapore Publishers.

20 Muscat, 1994, op. cit.

21 Muscat, 1994, op. cit.

22 The World Bank, 1993, p. 85.

23 Muscat, 1994, op. cit.

24 Muscat, 1994, op. cit. P. 124.

25 P. Phongpaichit, " Nu Nit, Noi and Thailand's Informal sector in Rapid Growth", in Chira Hongladarom and Shigeru Itoga eds., *Human Resources Deveopment Strategy in Thailand*, 1991, Tokyo, Institute of Developing Economies, pp. 89-111.

26 Muscat, 1994, op. cit.

27 The World Bank, 1993, op. cit.

28 A. Atkinson and C. Vorratnchaiphan, "Urban Environmental Management in Changing Development Context: The Case of Thailand", *Third World planning Review*, 1994, vol. 16, no. 2.

29 M. Douglas and M. Zoghlin, "Sustaining Cities at the Grassroots: Livelihood, Environment and Social Networks in Suan Phlu, Nabgkok, *Third World Planning Review*, vol. 16, no. 2, pp. 171-200.

30 Muscat, 1994, op. cit.

31 Muscat, 1994, op. cit. pp. 230-66.

32 Muscat, 1994, op. cit. p. 291.

33 Ibid.

34 U. Kaothien and D. Webster, " The Proposed Development Frame for the Core
Area of the Bangkok Metropolitan Region During the Eighth Plan Period (1997-
2001), chapter presented at the *International Seminar on Human Settlements
Policy*, 1995, Tokyo. P. 17.

35 Guillouet, 1990, op. cit. P. 57.

36 Muscat, 1994, op. cit.

37 P. Pakkasem, 1994, op. cit.

38 SAARC stands for South Asian Association for Regional Cooperation.

References

Amin, A.T.M.N., *A Policy Agenda for the Informal Sector in Thailand, HSD
Research Report* No. 30, 1994, Bangkok: HSD/AIT.

Amin, A.T.M.N., "Bangkok's Informal Sector and Slums Through the Thai
Economic Growth and Prosperity", chapter presented at the International Seminar
on *Human Settlements Policy, 1995: Settlements Problems in Metropolitan Core
Areas*, 1995b, 9-10 March, Tokyo, 18pp.

Atkinson, Adrian and Vorratnchaiphan, Chamniern P., "Urban Environmental
Management in a Changing Development Context: The Case of Thailand", *Third
World Planning Review,* 1994, vol.16, no.2, pp. 148-169.

Douglass, M. and Zoghlin, M., "Sustaining Cities at the Grassroots: Livelihood, Env-
iron and Social Networks in Suan Phlu, Bangkok", *Third World Planning
Review,* 1994, vol. 16, no. 2 , May, pp. 171-200.

ESCAP, 1984. *Human Settlements Atlas for Asia and The Pacific,* Bangkok: UN-
ESCAP.

ESCAP, *State of Urbanization in Asia and the Pacific,* 1993, Bangkok: UN-
ESCAPE.

Guillouet, Alain, *Booming Economics of South East Asia: Thailand, Malaysia,
Singapore, Malaysia,* Singapore, 1990, Longman Singapore Publishers.

Ikemoto, Y. *Income Distribution: Its Changes, Causes and Structure,* 1991, Tokyo:
Institute of Developing Economies.

Kaothien, Utis and Webster, Douglas, "The Proposed development Frame for the
Core Area of the Bangkok Metropolitan Region During the Eighth Plan Period ,
1997-2001, chapter presented at *the International Seminar on Human Settlements
Policy,* 1995, 9-10 March, Tokyo, 17pp.

Korff, Rudigar, *Bangkok: Urban System and Everyday Life,* 1986, Saarbrucken, Fort Lauderdale: Verlay Breitenbach Publishers.

Mills, Edwin S., "Prospects for Growth and Urbanization in Thailand", chapter presented at SASIN Business School in Chulalongkorn University, 1989, Bangkok.

Mills, Edwin S. And Hamilton, B. W., *Urban Economics,* 1987, Glenview: Scott, Faresman Co.

Muscat, Robert, J., *The Fifth Tiger: A Study of Thai Development Policy,* 1994, Tokyo: United Nations University Press.

Pakkasem, Phisit, *Leading Issues in Thailand's Development Transformation,* 1988, Bangkok: National Economic and Social Development Board.

Phongpaichit, Pasuk, "Nu, Nit, Noi and Thailand's Informal Sector in Rapid Growth" in Chira Hongladarom and Shigeru Itoga (eds.), *Human Resources Development Strategy in Thailand,* 1991, Tokyo: Institute of Developing Economies, pp. 89-111.

Ratanakomut, Somchai; Ashakul, Charuma; and Krinanda, Thienchay, "Urban Poverty in Thailand: Critical Issues and Policy Measures", *Asian Development Review,* 1994, vol.12 no. 1, pp. 204-224.

Siamwalla, Ammar, *Land Abundant Agricultural Growth and Some of Its Consequences: The Case of Thailand,* 1990, Bangkok:TDRI.

The World Bank, *The East Asian Miracle: Economic Growth and Public Policy,* 1993, Washington D.C., World Bank.

.... *The World Development Report,* 1994, Washington D.C.

For Product Safety Concerns and Information please contact our EU
representative GPSR@taylorandfrancis.com Taylor & Francis Verlag GmbH,
Kaufingerstraße 24, 80331 München, Germany

Printed and bound by CPI Group (UK) Ltd, Croydon, CR0 4YY
08/05/2025
01864370-0011